Living Volume Two:

Growing in the

"YES"

of *God*

ABOUT THE AUTHOR

Rev. Dr. Derry James-Tannariello is Board Certified with the Association of Professional Chaplains, and carries a BA in Religion; BS in Personal Ministries and Psychology; MA in Christian Psychology; Master of Divinity; and Doctor of Ministry specializing in Christian Counseling. She has also been awarded VIP Woman of the Year with the National Association of Professional Women.

She was the founder of Chaplain Services at Sierra Nevada Memorial Hospital in California. Hospitals, churches, educational institutions and other community organizations solicit her expertise in training others to minister to the sick and terminally ill, and for help dealing with loss and grief.

Derry is an active chaplain, author, and sought-after speaker known for her compassionate heart, humor and life-changing inspirational stories of faith and wisdom. She is an internationally recognized seminar and workshop presenter and an interdenominational guest speaker and lecturer on topics of How to Have an Effective Prayer Life, Personal Transformation, Relational God, Spirituality and Health and many more spiritually uplifting topics.

She also speaks and presents seminars on Spiritual Support in Palliative Care, Bereavement and Grief, End of Life, Ministering to Our Dying Loved Ones, Effective Hospital Visitation and other topics in Hospital ministry.

Derry resides in New Hampshire with her husband, where she continues her Chaplaincy work as well as Spiritual Guidance and Pastoral Responsibilities.

She is the author of *Heaven Touches Earth: Handbook for Supporting Sick and Terminally Ill* and *Heaven Touches Earth: Scripture Travel Companion*. To learn more about other books written by Derry or to have her as a speaker for your event, workshop, or organization, visit her website:

FreedomInSurrender.net

LIVING VOLUME TWO:

Growing in the

"YES"

of God

Derry James-Tannariello, DMin BCC

For all the promises of God in Him ARE
yes, and in Him Amen ...
—2 Corinthians 1:20

Freedom in Surrender Publishing

Publisher's Cataloging-in-Publication Data
    James-Tannariello, Derry
        Living Vol. 2 : Growing in the "YES" of God / by Derry James-Tannariello, DMin
            BCC.—1st ed.
        p. cm.
    Includes bibliographical references.
    ISBN-13: 978-0-9980152-1-7
    ISBN-10: 0-9980152-1-0
    1. Prayer. 2. Pastoral Theology. 3. Worship. 4. God-Christianity.
    5. Jesus Christ. 6. Holy Spirit. I. James-Tannariello, Derry. II. Title.

Library of Congress Control Number: 2017939654

The author assumes full responsibility for the accuracy and interpretation of the Ellen White quotations cited in this publication.

The basis of the material herein has been taken from The Positive Way Syllabus and used with the permission of Robert Lee Law.

Printed in the United States of America

Credits:
Cover and graphics design by Teresa Troy, www.VCADesign.com
Interior design by: Ann Cuddy, acc922@comcast.net

Picture credits:
Cover photo, chapter head backgrounds: © by Dr. Derry James-Tannariello

Unless otherwise noted, scripture are taken from New King James Version (NKJV) 1982 by Thomas Nelson, Inc., (Public Domain)

Scripture marked RSV are taken from the Revised Standard Version of the Bible, copyright © 1946, 1952, and 1971 the Division of Christian Education of the National Council of the Churches of Christ in the United States of America. Used by permission. All rights reserved.

Scripture marked NIV are taken from THE HOLY BIBLE, NEW INTERNATIONAL VERSION®, NIV® Copyright © 1973, 1978, 1984, 2011 by Biblica, Inc.® Used by permission. All rights reserved worldwide.

To order *Growing in the "YES" of God*, or any other titles by this author, visit:
FreedomInSurrender.net

For information regarding quantity discount for bulk purchases for sales promotion, fund-raising, and education needs, contact the author at:
DerryTannar@gmail.com or (603) 232-8497
Visit the author's website at FreedomInSurrender.net

Whereby are given unto us exceeding great and precious promises: that by these ye might be partakers of the divine nature, having escaped the corruption that is in the world through lust.

—2 Peter 1:4 KJV

DEDICATION

Above all, anything I do, I dedicate to God—the Trinity, and I pray that they will be exalted and that the glory would be for the Kingdom. Without the enabling and miracles of intervention that have come from the throne of grace, I would never be able to complete such a project.

Secondly, if it had not been for the dedication and commitment of Bob and Elsie Law, and their devotion to the Lord, their love and desire for others to experience God as they have learned to do, I would not have lived a life of adventure with Jesus and the understanding of His love for me personally; a love that has carried me through every heartache and every joy.

It is because of this training and the consistent application in my life, that I too am anxious to share so that others may grow in Jesus. There are many who are desirous of a closer relationship and deeper walk with our Lord and Savior Jesus Christ. It is for you that this study is being presented. It is for self-study and then to be used in a group. If we impart what we learn, it helps us retain it and strengthens our habits of application. These lessons are tried and true!

I also dedicate this study to the thousands of students over the past 40 years that have taken this course and proven its truth, value, and applicability to life and growth in Jesus. They were faithful in their attendance, and diligently and expectantly completed their homework incorporating it as a part of their life. Their stories, commitment, and encouragement to put the lessons into book form have been an inspiration.

I also dedicate this study guide to my husband, mother, sisters, treasured sons, and those in my church and community who have walked the journey of life with me—both good and difficult and for their support and love.

"Amazing? Yes! We capture how Abram must have felt as he began to walk through the promise God had made. To claim what God has offered is our challenge. We live as spiritual paupers when unlimited resources are placed at our disposal. There is nothing left out. All we need, now and for eternity, has been given to us."

—Lloyd Ogilvie

CONTENTS

Contents

FOREWORD

This course has been rewritten with additions to the original syllabus *"Positive Way"* compiled and written by Bob and Elsie Law and used with their permission. Of this course, Edwin Zackrison, Associate Professor of Religion at Southern Missionary College, stated:

> In this course you will walk with the living, dynamic Christ. Jesus, as a human being, lived on this earth and faced life as you and I face it. He died to give us "authority to become children of God." John 1:12. He wishes for us to have victory over the flesh, the world, and the devil (Matthew. 4:1-11), and He has not revealed this wish as an idle platitude. What God promises, He also provides in Christ Jesus (2 Corinthians 1:20) at the cross, in the application of His merits to us via forgiveness (Romans 4:7-8), and in the sanctified life. He is our "wisdom, our righteousness (justification) and sanctification and redemption" (1 Corinthians 1:30).

Growing in the "YES" of God

"He is not the God of the 'half-empty' or the 'half-full' in our lives.
He is the God of the 'Exceeding abundantly above all we could ask or think.'
His will for us is not just 'joy' but 'great joy'
    … not just 'peace' but the 'peace that passes all understanding'
    … not just 'love' but 'fullness of love'
    … not just to be a conqueror but to be 'more than a conqueror.'
When He fills our cup, it is overflowing. When He flows through us, it is as rivers of living water.
When He meets a need, He does it out of the riches that are in Christ."

—Roy Lessin,
Always Loved, Never Forgotten

ACKNOWLEDGEMENTS

God has shown His interest and approval for **Living Volume One** and **Two** on numerous occasions. His interventions have validated the Holy Spirit's call and direction. I have been overjoyed and encouraged to experience how God has orchestrated so many particulars in order to accomplish His ends for these books. I refer to these as "*Kisses from Heaven.*"

I was busily involved with **Living Volume One**, when a delightful gentleman approached me at church. He said, "I understand you need me." Quite surprised, I responded, "I do? How so?" He smiled and said, "I hear you're writing a book. I'm an editor."

Wow!!! I had no idea how much I needed Ray Fusci. He not only guided me through the processes but brought amazing ideas and detail into it. He took over *Living Volume One: Praying in the "Yes" of God* and put all my work in a presentation that we both can be proud of. Thank you Ray for your generous and unselfish heart.

Then there is Ann Cuddy, a precious sister to me. An amazing gifted woman that from the first hearing of my writings has been by my side helping, encouraging, working on my website, doing research for me, and a host of other accomplishments and contributions that I am unable to enumerate. She is the one responsible for formatting *Living Volume Two: Growing in the "Yes" of God*, and making my books available. I thank you so, so much Ann and just love you to pieces.

Then our design artist changed positions and became unavailable. I now am blessed to have Teresa Troy, VCA Designs as part of our team. What a sweet spirit she has.

And to my faithful friend, Laura Andrews, who checked each text and made sure the references were correct. Our Laura, who always goes the extra mile; love and hugs "Smiley!"

So, all of this publishing a book is not an easy process; and it is costly. I need to reimburse these precious people for using their talents to bless me; despite their generosity. But as a now per diem Chaplain, funds are not readily available. That is no problem for God. Just when I thought we were going to have to close everything down, God provided unexpected funds. He has provided in a number of ways; but for this book, I would especially like to thank Mary Ann Matson, an author herself, for her monetary donations, faith in me, and encouragement through the Holy Spirit.

So today, as you open **Volume One** and/or **Volume Two** of **Living**, know that God has put the pieces together ... even providing the pictures for the covers. Pictures that I took vacationing with my husband in Florida a number of years ago seemed to project the feel of the contents ... and moving forward with Jesus.

To each person who has played a part in the publishing of these two books, *Living Volume: One-Praying in the "Yes" of God*, and *Living Volume Two: Growing in the "Yes" of God,* I give my heartfelt thanks and pray that God will abundantly bless them continually.

How to Use This Book

It is our hope that the power, the meaning, the force of this text will become very real and very precious to you as you work through this study.

2 Peter 1:4 says, *Through these He has given us great and precious promises, so that through them you may participate in the divine nature, having escaped the corruption in the world caused by evil desires.*

Please notice the word "promises" because it is one of the keywords of this verse. "Divine nature" are the other two keywords. Here we have a precious promise in this text that tells us that you and I today do not have to lead lives of failure. We do not have to lead lives of defeat or frustration. This text tells us that we may become partakers of the divine nature of God in our heart and in our life. This text not only tells you what you can have, but how you can have it.

According to our *Bible*, the way we can become partakers of the divine nature is through the promises of God's word. There are over 7000 of them. Anyone can learn to know which promise is applicable, then claim it, and appropriate it in daily living. You can then have the entire power and resources of heaven at your disposal to help you live the kind of life the Christ wants you to live. That's what Christianity is all about. This is what the gospel message is all about—to become partakers of the divine nature. In this study you will not only learn how to live a victorious Christian life, how to be successful in soul winning and counseling, but how to have peace of mind. In short, you will learn how to take God at his word.

You will get the most understanding as well as develop life-changing habits if you work straight through the material from beginning to end. We recommend that you take a chapter a week, or take two weeks if you need to. Do **all** the assignments in the chapters and experience **"Growing"** in Jesus and the power of His word.

We always retain more, and "settle" what we have learned with application and sharing. After you have completed this study we strongly encourage you to share with others. It will be easy for you to get an interested group together, because you have been sharing your excitement and enthusiasm as you have been going through each study. You can't help yourself!

Growing in the "YES" of God

You will be the facilitator. You will become their mentor, teacher, leader, because you are now the one with experience and have a notebook full of answers to prayer and testimonies to validate each teaching. Have them get a copy of *Living Volume One: Praying in the "Yes" of God*, and this study manual, *Living Volume Two: Growing in the "Yes" of God*. Meet once a week as you work through the books again. Follow the format/instructions found in Appendix B, **Leaders and Teachers Guide**.

Each student who completes the study is now in a position to begin a new group as the facilitator with exciting testimonies to share. Our prayer is that anyone desirous of the knowledge and experience of Jesus as a personal Savior; Jesus, Who cares about us intimately and is anxious to answer our prayers and prove Himself real, will finally have that opportunity. When God calls, He enables. How many jewels will you have in your crown? This is a fun and easy way to share Jesus with others and enjoy the excitement of watching them "grow."

INTRODUCTION

Whereby are given unto us exceeding great and precious promises: that by these ye might be partakers of the divine nature, having escaped the corruption that is in the world through lust.—2 Peter 1:4

"Those who exercise little faith now, are in the greatest danger of falling under the power of satanic delusions and the decree to compel the conscience. And even if they endure the test, they will be plunged into deeper distress and anguish in the time of trouble, because they have never made it a habit to trust in God. The lessons of faith which they have neglected they will be forced to learn under a terrible pressure of discouragement. We should now acquaint ourselves with God by proving His promises,"[1] and by developing a personal relationship with Him through personalizing scripture.

We should be more concerned about believing than with seeing or feeling. "The nobleman wanted to see the fulfillment of his prayer before he should believe; but he had to accept the word of Jesus that his request was heard and the blessing granted. This lesson we also have to learn. Not because we see or feel that God hears us are we to believe. We are to trust in His promises. When we come to Him in faith, we should believe that we receive it, and thank Him that we have received it. Then we are to go about our duties, assured that the blessing will be realized when we need it most. When we have learned to do this, we shall know that our prayers are answered. God will do for us *exceeding, abundantly, according to the riches of His glory*, and the working of His mighty power.—Ephesians 3:20, 16, 1:19.[2]

*(Before beginning this course, please read pages xvii – 16 of **Living Volume One: Praying in the "YES" of God**.)*

Growing in the "YES" of God

1. **OBJECTIVES OF THIS COURSE**

   a. To emphasize the great need of God's people for effective prayer life.

   b. To prove that God stands behind His word and He can be trusted.

   c. To confirm that miracles are not outdated.

   d. To recognize Christ as our personal Friend and Savior and realize His interest in each detail of our lives.

   e. To demonstrate the reality of the **Prayer of Faith**, especially the **Prayer of Reception**, by active experimentation.

   f. To help develop a deeper relationship with God through application of the conditions to answered prayer and an understanding of the **divine science of prayer**.

   g. To recognize that adventure with Jesus equals peace of mind.

   h. To understand how problems can reveal opportunities.

   i. To simplify witnessing/making disciples as a way of life.

2. **BENEFITS OF THIS COURSE**

   Write out the scriptures below. By claiming the promises of God and appropriating them to our daily lives, we can:

   a. Have an effective prayer life, experiencing many personal blessings.
   John 16:24

   _____

   b. See how the power of God's word becomes a power in our lives as we apply it.
   Psalm 119:105

   _____

   c. Learn to put our confidence in God rather than man.
   Psalm 118:8

   _____

d. Have assurance of Christ's love for us personally.
    1 John 3:1

_____

e. Experience the reality of living and praying by faith in Jesus. (Read Hebrews 11)
    John 14:13

_____

f. Develop a character like Jesus.
    2 Peter 1:4-8

_____

_____

_____

g. Have peace of mind.
    Isaiah 26:3

_____

h. Apply a positive approach to life.
    Philippians 4:6, 13

_____

i. Become effective witnesses by "demonstrating" what the Christ has done in our life and what He can do daily.
    Proverbs 11:25

_____

j. Our role as channels of the Holy Spirit through living and interceding.
    John 14:26

_____

"Two of the most obvious side effects of spending time with our Lord, and doing things 'His way,' are a transformed life and a growing love for our Savior."
—Derry

"Faith is needed in the smaller no less than in the greater experiences of life. In all our daily interests and occupations the sustaining strength of God becomes real to us through an abiding trust."

—Education, p. 255

LESSON ONE—THE PRAYER OF FAITH

Now faith is the assurance of things hoped for, the conviction of things not seen.

—Hebrews 11:1 ESV

(Please refer to pages 17-20 in **Living Volume One: Praying in the "YES" of God** *before studying this chapter.)*

Our communication with God is expressed by various types of praying as presented below. Each is a different expression of prayer with a defined focus. All are important and should be part of communing with our most Holy and Exalted Lord. Out of the types presented here, our focal point will be mainly on the application and effectiveness of the **Prayer of Faith/Reception**.

(Please refer to pages 27-35 in **Living Volume One: Praying in the "YES" of God** *before you study the followings section.)*

Types of Prayer
Study the examples given in the following scriptures regarding the different types of prayer.

Prayer of Reverence and Adoration—Psalm 147

Prayer of Thanksgiving—Psalm 118

Prayer of Dedication—1 Samuel 1:11

Prayer of Faith (also called Petition)—Daniel 9:4-19, John 17:1-26

Prayer of Reception—Matthew 21:22, 1 John 5:14, 15

Prayer of Commitment—Luke 22:42, Mark 14:36

Prayer of Intercession—John 17

PRAYER OF FAITH
(Also called prayer of **"Reception"** and **"Petition"**)

Many years ago, there was an old farmer. He rode his horse everywhere he went, and found the horse to be a very effective means of transportation for him. When his neighbor drove by in his new car, the farmer wasn't even tempted. He loved his horse.

One day the horse became very sick and badly in need of a veterinarian; now the farmer was stuck. He had no way to get to town for help. While he was contemplating his dilemma he noticed his neighbor coming around the corner some ways from his pasture. He quickly ran out to flag him down. After explaining his predicament, he found himself accepting the invitation to ride in the passenger seat of this new invention to get the vet.

After his ride in the car, he realized that though his horse could get him most places he wanted to go, there was a more effective means of transportation. That is how it is when we understand the "*divine science of prayer.*" There is a more effective means of communication that opens the windows of heaven—**Praying in the "Yes" of God.** It is imperative that we understand the **"Prayer of Faith/Reception"** and God's conditions to answered **prayer**.

Principles regarding the connection of Faith and Prayer

1. The *"science of prayer"* is the exercise of **faith** in connection with prayer.
2. **Prayer** and **faith** are closely associated.
3. Wavering **faith** or doubt cannot expect prayers to be answered.

Elements of Petition

Use the acronym **BASE** to help you remember these key elements.

B Belief: *Therefore I tell you, whatever you **ask** in prayer, **believe** that you receive it, and you will.*—Mark 11:24 ESV

A Ask: *And even now I know that whatever You **ask** from God, He will grant it to You.*—John 11:22 AMPC

It is a part of God's plan to grant us in answer to the **prayer of faith** that which He would not bestow did we not thus ask."[3]

S Science: (Conditions) "In the **Prayer of Faith** (Petition and Reception), there is a divine **science**; it is a **science** that everyone who would make his lifework a success must understand."[4]

E Expectancy: "The **prayer** that comes from an earnest heart, when the simple wants of the soul are expressed just as we would ask an earthly friend for a favor, **expecting** that it would be granted—this is the prayer of **faith**."[5]

"There is greater encouragement for us in the least blessing we ourselves receive from God than in all the accounts we can read of the **faith** and experience of others."[6]

Types of Petitions

PRAYER OF COMMITTMENT

This type of **prayer** will be covered in another chapter. This **prayer** is to be **prayed** when we are not sure of God's will, as Christ **prayed**, *Not as I will, but as Thou wilt.*—Matthew 26:39 KJV. We may feel in ourselves that

Growing in the "YES" of God

things should be a certain way, but God may have a different way; we therefore commit our will to His.

PRAYER OF RECEPTION

*(Please refer to pgs 96-104 in **Living Volume One: Praying in the "YES" of God**, while you are studying this section.)*

This is a **prayer** that is much neglected. We **pray** claiming a simple *Bible* text regarding what God has clearly promised; ***Praying in the "YES" of God*** with expectation and faith.

Look up **2 Corinthians 1:20** and paraphrase it here: _____

_____

1. We are to ask, believe and give thanks that we have received those things promised.

   As soon as we **ask**, God begins working on the answer: "For the pardon of sin, for the Holy Spirit, for a Christlike temper, for wisdom and strength to do His work, for any gift He has promised, we may **ask**; then we are to **believe** that we **receive** and return **thanks** to God that we have **received**."[7]

   "It is the will of God to cleanse us from sin, to make us His children and to enable us to live a holy life. So we may **ask** for these blessings and **believe** that we **receive** them, and **thank** God that we have **received** them."[8]

2. We are to understand that the gift is in the promise.

   Whatever gift He promises, is in the promise itself. The seed is the word of God.—Luke 8:11 As surely as the oak is in the acorn, so surely is the gift of God in His promise. If we receive the promise, we have the gift."[9]

3. We are to find subject matter for prayer in the promises.

   "Every promise in the Word of God furnishes us with subject matter for prayer, presenting the pledged Word of Jehovah as our assurance."[10] *God is not a man that He should lie.*—Numbers 23:19

How to Pray the Prayer of Reception (Faith, Petition)

*(Please refer to pages 97-101 in **Living Volume One: Praying in the "YES" of God** while you are studying this section.)*

The verbal conditions—Look up and write out the following Scriptures:

ASK: Matthew 7:7 NIV

_____

BELIEVE: Mark 11:24 NIV

_____

THANK: Colossians 4:2

_____

Assignment

1. Pray the following prayers

The following **prayers** should be **prayed** once or twice a day. You will want to establish the habit of daily asking for the Holy Spirit to fill you, direct you, and use you.

You will want to remember to intercede in behalf of others. As you establish these habits, you are also incorporating the components of **asking**, **believing**, and **thanking** God into your **prayers**. We **thank** God immediately, because when we **pray**, He begins working on the answer. Often those things you **pray** for were put in your heart by Him, because He already has an answer waiting.

There is nothing sacred about these exact words. The suggestions here are just to help you remember the necessity of complying with God's instructions and including these elements as you petition God's blessings. This is a guide to familiarize you with the **Prayer of Reception**. If this approach is new to you, keep these examples handy until you are well acquainted with the concept and it becomes a part of your life.

Daily Prayer Sheet

For Forgiveness

Dear Heavenly Father,

I **ask** that You will forgive me for _____;

I **believe** that You have forgiven me because You have promised in 1 John 1:9;

I **thank** You that You have forgiven me.

In Jesus' name, Amen.

For Intercession and Soul Winning

Dear Heavenly Father,

I **ask** that You will give me life to give _____;

I **believe** that You are giving me life to give him/her because You have promised in 1 John 5:16;

I **thank** You that You have given me life to give him/her.

In Jesus' name, Amen.

For the Holy Spirit

Dear Heavenly Father,

I **ask** that You will give me the Holy Spirit;

I **believe** that You are giving me the Holy Spirit because You have promised in Luke 11:13;

I **thank** You that You have given me the Holy Spirit.

In Jesus' name, Amen.

2. **Begin claiming promises for personal needs**

Begin claiming **promises** for personal needs as part of your daily **prayer** time, placing the problems and **promises** on the **Record of Experiences** sheet at the end of this chapter.

It is important to **pray** the **promises** set out in God's Word. **Ask** the Holy Spirit to reveal the **promises** you need and to guide your thoughts as you record your personal **promises** for your life matters. You will find additional pages of the **Record of Experiences** at the end of this book. Feel free to copy and print as many copies as you need. You will also find a downloadable page on our website: FreedomInSurrender.net. Below are some suggested promises to get you started.

These are some of His **promises** you can use for your own daily problems of life:

For forgiveness of sin	1 John 1:9
For the fruit of the Spirit	Galatians 5:22-23
For instruction and guidance by God	Psalm 32:8-11
For peace of mind	Isaiah 26:3
For your own personal needs	Philippians 4:19
For heaven's windows to be opened	Malachi 3:10-12
For Divine wisdom	James 1:5-8

James 1:5-8 may also be used for wisdom to find a particular **promise** to fit your need. While there are over 7000 **promises** found in the *Bible*, a list, though not exhaustive, of **promises** can be found in Appendix A.

3. Read daily *Christ is Our Example* on the following page.
4. Read *Faith and Prayer* at the end of this chapter
5. Journal on your **Reflections** page

You may use your own journal to record your journey. If you are not accustomed to journaling, we have included a **Reflections** page at the end of each chapter of this Study. We strongly encourage you to use this page to write about what you've learned that week. You might journal on how the reading of *Christ as Our Example* changed you and your approach to life and/or some of the important points that spoke to you from your reading *Faith and Prayer*.

Perhaps you will want to record what you heard from God this week on your **Reflections** page, or maybe what you are not hearing. Maybe you have come across a Promise verse that would be beneficial to someone else. What questions or answers did this week's lesson provoke? This is your reflections page. While you are encouraged to share all that God is doing in your life, know that its contents are private, for you to share as you feel comfortable.

Christic is Our Example

We are forming characters for heaven. No character can be complete without trial and suffering. We must be tested. We must be tried. Christ bore the test of character in our behalf, that we might bear this test in our own behalf, through the divine strength He has brought to us. Christ is our example in patience, in forbearance in meekness and lowliness of mind. He was at variance and at war with the whole ungodly world; yet He did not give way to passion and violence manifested in words and actions, although receiving shameful abuse in return for good works. He was afflicted. He was rejected and despitefully treated, yet He retaliated not. He possessed self-control, dignity and majesty. He suffered with calmness and for abuse gave only compassion, pity and love.

Imitate your Redeemer in these things. Do not get excited when things go wrong. Do not let self arise, and lose your self-control because you fancy things are not as they should be. Because others are wrong is no excuse for you to do wrong. Two wrongs will not make one right. You have victories to gain in order to overcome as Christ overcame.

Christ never murmured, never uttered discontent, displeasure, or resentment. He was never disheartened, discouraged, ruffled or fretted. He was patient, calm, and self-possessed under the most exciting and trying circumstances. All His works were performed with a quiet dignity and ease, whatever commotion was around Him. Applause did not elate Him. He feared not the threats of His enemies. He moved amid the world of excitement, of violence and crime, as the sun moves above the clouds. Human passions and commotions and trials were beneath Him. He sailed like the sun above them all. Yet He was not indifferent to the woes of men. His heart was ever touched with the sufferings and necessities of His brethren, as though He Himself was the one afflicted. He had a calm inward joy, a peace which was serene. His will was ever swallowed up in the will of His Father. Not My will but Thine be done, was heard from His pale and quivering lips.[11]

Faith and Prayer

Faith is trusting God—believing that He loves us and knows best what is for our good. Thus it leads us to choose His way instead of our own. In place of our ignorance, it accepts His wisdom; in place of our weakness, His strength; in place of our sinfulness, His righteousness. Our lives are already His; faith acknowledges His ownership and accepts its blessing. Truth, uprightness, purity, have been pointed out as secrets of life's success. Faith puts us in possession of these principles.

Every good impulse or aspiration is the gift of God. Faith receives from God the life that alone can produce true growth and efficiency.

Make very plain how to exercise faith. To every promise of God there are conditions. If we are willing to do His will, all His strength is ours. Whatever gift He promises is in the promise itself. *The seed is the word of God.*—Luke 8:11. As surely as the oak is in the acorn, so surely is the gift of God in His promise. If we receive the promise, we have the gift.

Faith that enables us to receive God's gifts is itself a gift, of which some measure is imparted to every human being. It grows as it is exercised in appropriating the Word of God. In order to strengthen faith, we must often bring it into contact with the Word.

In the study of the *Bible* the student should be led to see the power of God's word. In the creation, *He spoke, and it was done; He commanded, and it stood fast.* He *calls those things which do not exist as though they did*—Psalm 33:9; Romans 4:17, for when He calls them, they are.

The World's True Nobility

How often those who trusted the word of God have withstood the power of the whole world—Enoch, holding fast his faith in the triumph of righteousness against a corrupt and scoffing generation; Noah and his household against people of his time, men and women of the greatest physical and mental strength and the most debased in morals; the children of Israel at the Red Sea, a helpless, terrified multitude of slaves, against the mightiest army of the mightiest nation on the globe; David, a shepherd boy, having God's promise of the throne, against Saul, the established monarch, determined to hold fast his power; Shadrach and his companions in the fire, and Nebuchadnezzar on the throne; Daniel among the lions, his enemies in the high places of the kingdom; Jesus on the cross,

9

and the Jewish priests and rulers forcing even the Roman governor to work their will; Paul in chains led to a criminal's death, Nero the despot.

Such examples are found not only in the *Bible* but abound in every record of human progress. The Vaudois and the Huguenots, Wycliffe and Huss, Jerome and Luther, Tyndale and Knox, Zinzendorf and Wesley, with multitudes of others, have witnessed to the power of God's word against human power and policy in support of evil. These are the world's true nobility. This is its royal line. In this line young people of today are called to take their places.

Faith is needed in the smaller no less than in the greater experiences of life. In all our daily interests and occupations the sustaining strength of God becomes real to us through an abiding trust.

Viewed from its human side, life is an untried path. In regard to our deeper experiences, we each walk alone. Into our inner life no other human being can fully enter. As little children set forth on that journey, how earnest should be the effort to direct their trust to the sure Guide and Helper!

As a shield from temptation and an inspiration to purity and truth, no other influence can equal the sense of God's presence. *All things are naked and open to the eyes of Him to whom we must give account.* He is *of purer eyes than to behold evil, and cannot look on wickedness.*—Hebrews 4:13; Habakkuk 1:13. This thought was Joseph's shield amidst the corruptions of Egypt. To the allurements of temptation his answer was steadfast: *How ... can I do this great wickedness, and sin against God?*—Genesis 39:9. Faith, if cherished, will provide that shield to every soul.

Only the sense of God's presence can banish the fear that, for timid children, would make life a burden. Help them to fix in memory the promise, *The angel of the Lord encamps all around those who fear Him, and delivers them.*—Psalm 34:7. Have them read that wonderful story of Elisha in the mountain city, with a mighty encircling band of heavenly angels between him and the hosts of armed men. Tell them how God's angel appeared to Peter, in prison and condemned to death; how, past the armed guards, the massive doors and great iron gateway with their bolts and bars, the angel led God's servant forth in safety.

Picture for them that scene on the sea, when Paul the prisoner, on his way to trial and execution, spoke those grand words of courage and hope: "I urge you to take heart, for there will be no loss of life among you. ... For there stood by me this night an angel of the God to whom I belong and whom I serve, saying, *Do not be afraid, Paul; you must be brought before Caesar; and, indeed, God has granted you all those who sail with you.* So, because there was in that ship one man through whom God could work, the whole shipload of heathen soldiers and sailors was preserved. *They all escaped safely to land.*—Acts 27:22-24, 44.

These things were written not merely that we might read and wonder, but that the same faith which worked in God's servants of old might work in us. In no less marked a manner than He worked then will He work now wherever there are hearts of faith to be channels of His power. Teach the self-distrustful, whose lack of self-reliance leads them to shrink from care and responsibility, to rely upon God. Thus many a person who otherwise would be but a cipher in the world, perhaps only a helpless burden, will be able to say with the apostle Paul, *I can do all things through Christ who strengthens me.*—Philippians 4:13.

God Is the Guardian of Right

For the child who is quick to resent injuries, faith has precious lessons. The disposition to resist evil or to avenge wrong is often prompted by a keen sense of justice and an active, energetic spirit. Children should be taught that God is the eternal guardian of right. He has a tender care for the beings whom He so loved as to give His dearest Beloved to save. He will deal with every wrongdoer.

He who touches you touches the apple of His eye.—Zechariah 2:8. *Commit your way to the Lord, trust also in Him, and He shall bring it to pass. ... He shall bring forth your righteousness as the light, and your justice as the noonday.*—Psalm 37:5, 6.

Those who know Your name will put their trust in You; for You, Lord, have not forsaken those who seek You.—Psalm 9:10.

The compassion that God manifests toward us, He tells us to manifest toward others. Encourage the impulsive, the self-sufficient, and the revengeful, to behold the meek and lowly One, led as a lamb to the slaughter, unretaliating as a sheep before its shearer's. Point them to Him whom our sins have pierced and our sorrows burdened, and they will learn to endure, to forbear, and to forgive.

Through faith in Christ every deficiency of character may be supplied, every defilement cleansed, every fault corrected, every excellence developed. *You are complete in Him.*—Colossians 2:10.

Prayer and faith are closely allied, and they need to be studied together. In the prayer of faith there is a divine science, a science that everyone who would make his or her lifework a success must understand. Christ says, *Whatever things you ask when you pray, believe that you receive them, and you will have them.*—Mark 11:24. He makes it plain that our asking must be according to God's will. We must ask for the things He has promised, and whatever we receive must be used in doing His will. When the conditions have been met, the promise is unequivocal.

For the pardon of sin, for the Holy Spirit, for a Christ-like temper, for wisdom and strength to do His work, for any gift He has promised, we may ask; then we are to believe that we receive, and thank God that we have received. The gift is in the promise, and we may go about our work assured that the gift, which we already possess, will be realized when we need it most.

Prayer a Necessity

To live thus by the Word of God means the surrender to Him of the whole life. We will feel a continual sense of need and dependence, a drawing out of the heart after God. Prayer is a necessity, for it is the life of the soul. Family prayer, public prayer, have their place, but it is secret communion with God that sustains the soul life.

In the mount with God Moses saw the pattern of that wonderful building which was to be the abiding place of His glory. It is in the mount with God—in the secret place of communion—that we are to contemplate His glorious ideal for humanity. Thus we shall be enabled so to fashion our character building that to us may be fulfilled His promise, *I will dwell in them and walk among them. I will be their God, and they shall be My people.*—2 Corinthians 6:16.

It was in hours of solitary prayer that Jesus received wisdom and power. Encourage the young to follow His example in finding at dawn and twilight a quiet season for communion with their Father in heaven. And throughout the day let them lift up their hearts to God. At every step of our way He says, *I the Lord your God will hold your right hand, Fear not, I will help you.*—Isaiah 41:13.

These are lessons that only people who have learned them can teach. It is because so many parents and teachers profess to believe the Word of God while their lives deny its power, that the teaching of Scripture has no greater effect on children and youth. It is one thing to treat the *Bible* as a book of good moral instruction, to be followed so far as is consistent with the spirit of the times and our position in the world, it is another thing to regard it as it really is—the Word of the living God, the Word that is our life, the Word that is to mold our actions, our words, and our thoughts. To hold God's Word as anything less than this is to reject it. And this rejection by those who profess to believe it, is foremost among the causes of skepticism and infidelity in today's youth.

Take Time With God

Unprecedented intensity is taking possession of the world. In amusement, in moneymaking, in the contest for power, in the very struggle for existence, there is a terrible force that engrosses body and mind and soul. In the midst of this maddening rush, God is speaking. He invites us to come apart and commune with Him. Be still, and know that I am God.—Psalm 46:10.

Many, even in their seasons of devotion, fail to receive the blessing of real communion with God. They are in too great haste. With hurried steps they press through the circle of Christ's loving presence, pausing perhaps a moment within the sacred precincts, but not waiting for counsel. They have no time to remain with the divine Teacher. With their burdens they return to their work.

These workers can never attain the highest success until they learn the secret of strength. They must give themselves time to think, to pray, to wait upon God for a renewal of physical, mental, and spiritual power. They need the uplifting influence of His Spirit. Receiving this, they will be quickened by fresh life. The wearied frame and tired brain will be refreshed, the burdened heart lightened.

Growing in the "YES" of God

Not just a pause for a moment in His presence, but personal contact with Christ—sitting down in companionship with Him—this is our need. What a great day it will be for the children of our homes and the students of our schools when parents and teachers learn in their own lives the precious experience pictured in these words by Solomon: *Like an apple tree among the trees of the woods, so is my beloved among the sons. I sat down in his shade with great delight, and his fruit was sweet to my taste. He brought me to the banqueting house, and his banner over me was love.*—Song of Solomon 2:3-4.[12]

Record of Experiences

Record of Experiences

This record of experiences will help you keep a list of the problems you had, the promises you claimed and the date your prayers were answered. It will help to increase your faith in the future when you can look back and see how God so miraculously intervened.

Date Asked	Problem	Promise Text	Date Answered	How Answered

Growing in the "YES" of God

Speak Lord, Your servant is listening—1 Samuel 3:9-10 NIV

Weekly Reflections

_____

_____

_____

_____

_____

_____

_____

_____

_____

_____

_____

_____

_____

"But to claim that prayer will always be answered in the very way and for the particular thing that we desire, is presumption."

—*Praying in the "YES" of God*, p. 22

LESSON TWO——FUNDAMENTAL PRINCIPLES AND PRESUMPTION

Keep back Your servant also from presumptuous sins; let them not have dominion over me!

—Psalm 19:13

*(Please refer to pages 21-24 in **Living Volume One: Praying in the "YES" of God** while you are studying this chapter.)*

God's **promises** are all about relationship. We need to get a hold of God.

"There are those who profess to serve God, while they rely upon their own efforts to obey His law, to form a right character, and secure salvation. Their hearts are not moved by any deep sense of love of Christ, but they seek to perform the duties of the Christian life as that which God requires of them in order to gain Heaven. Such religion is worth nothing.

When Christ dwells in the heart, the soul will be so filled with His love, with the joy of communion with Him, that it will cleave to Him; and in the contemplation of Him, self will be forgotten ... Those who feel the constraining love of God, do not ask how little may be given to meet the requirements of God; they do not ask for the lowest standard, but aim at perfect conformity to the will of their Redeemer. With earnest desire they yield all ... A profession of Christ without this deep love is mere talk, dry formality, and heavy drudgery.

Do you feel that it is too great a sacrifice to yield all to Christ? Ask yourself the question, "What has Christ given for me?" The Son of God gave all—life and love and suffering for our redemption. And can it be that we, be unworthy objects of so great love, will withhold our hearts from Him?"[13]

"The blessing comes when, by faith, the soul surrenders itself to God."[14]

The Story of Assurance
—Romans 4:13-25

Record your thoughts and insights:

_____

_____

_____

_____

_____

_____

What has Christ given me?

_____

_____

_____

_____

_____

_____

What now can I do for Him?

_____

_____

_____

_____

_____

Fundamental Principles

We need to understand some basic and fundamental gospel **principles** as we approach the subject of conditions.

1. **Every command of God is actually a promise.**

   "All of His (God's) biddings are enablings."[15] "Every **command** is a **promise**; accepted by the will, received into the soul, it brings with it the life of the Infinite One. It transforms the nature and recreates the soul in the image of God."[16] "In every **command** or injunction that God gives there is a **promise** the most positive underlying the **command**."[17]

   Read **Ezekiel 36:24-27** and paraphrase it here:

   _____

   _____

   _____

   If God asks us to do something, He will empower us to do it. So if He **commands** us to do something, He is **promising** to be with us to that end.

   God will clean us up and prepare our hearts to obey His **commands**—which He **promises** to fulfill in us. In every **command** that God gives is His **promise** of enabling; He never asks us to do anything He is not willing to help us do.

2. **God stands back of every promise He has given.**

   Read **Numbers 23:19** and paraphrase it here:

   _____

   Read **Hebrews 10:23** and paraphrase it here:

   _____

"God stands back of every **promise** He has made. The honor of His throne is staked for the fulfillment of His word to us."[18]

3. **The promises are available and plentiful.**

   Read **2 Corinthians 7:1** and paraphrase it here:

   _____

   _____

   It is said that there are over 7000 *Bible* promises, or clusters of promises. They cover every problem in life. "There is no limit to the usefulness of one who, putting self aside, makes room for the working of the Holy Spirit upon his heart and lives a life wholly consecrated to God."[19]

4. **Every promise of God is conditional.**
   (Read and study Jeremiah 18:1-11)

   Read **John 15:7** and paraphrase it here:

   _____

   _____

   This text shows that the condition for us to receive what we ask of God is to abide.

   > **Reflection Thoughts**—What does it mean to you to "Abide in Him?" Journal your thoughts on your weekly Reflections page

"There are **conditions** to the fulfillment of God's **promises**, and prayer can never take the place of duty. Those who bring their petitions to God, claiming His **promise** while they do not comply with the **conditions,** insult Jehovah."[20] "It should be remembered that the **promises** and threatenings of God are alike **conditional**."[21]

5. **Every victory will be gained only by surrendering the will to God's will.**

   Read **John 15:4-5** and paraphrase it here:

   _____

   _____

   Read **Colossians 3:33** and paraphrase it here:

   _____

   Whatever is to be done at His **command** may be accomplished in His strength. "All His biddings are enablings."[22] Jesus wants your affection, cheerful obedience, unconditional surrender and devotion to Him.

6. **We must cooperate with God—allow Him access to us.**

   Read **Mark 9:24** and paraphrase it here:

   _____

   _____

   "You are not able, of yourself, to bring your purposes and desires and inclinations into submission to the will of God; but if you are 'willing to be made willing,' God will accomplish the work for you."[23]

   "When it is in the heart to obey God, when efforts are put forth to this end, Jesus accepts this disposition and effort as man's best service, and He makes up for the deficiency with His own Divine merit." [24]

7. **Through the promises we may become partakers of the Divine nature.**

   Read **2 Peter 1:3-4** and paraphrase them here:

   _____

   _____

   "Every student should understand that the principles which he adopts become a living, molding influence upon character. He who accepts Christ as his personal Savior, will love Jesus, and all for whom Christ has died ... He will surrender himself without reservation to the rule of Christ."[25]

8. **Every sinful trait can be subdued, and every temptation resisted.**

   Read **John 1:12** and paraphrase it here:

   _____

   _____

   Read **1 Corinthians 10:13** and paraphrase it here:

   _____

   _____

   "Through faith in Christ, every deficiency of character may be supplied, every defilement cleansed, every fault corrected, every excellence developed,"[26] and every need fulfilled.

   "In Christ, God has provided means for subduing every sinful trait and resisting every temptation however strong."[27]

9. **We have no power of ourselves to fulfill the conditions.**

Read **Jeremiah 13:23** and paraphrase it here:

_____

_____

_____

We should understand clearly that fulfilling **conditions** is not accomplished through our power. It can only be done in our faith relationship with Christ.

Presumption

"Faith is in no sense allied to **presumption**. Only he who has true faith is secure against **presumption**. For **presumption** is Satan's counterfeit of faith. Faith claims God's **promises**, and brings forth fruit in obedience. **Presumption** also claims the **promises**, but uses them as Satan did, to excuse transgression. Faith would have led our first parents to trust the love of God, and obey His **commands**. **Presumption** led them to transgress His law, believing that His great love would save them from the consequences of their sin. It is not faith that claims the favor of Heaven without complying with the **conditions** on which mercy is to be granted. Genuine faith has its foundation in the promises and provisions of the Scriptures."[28]

Cautions and the Problem of "Presumption"

CAUTIONS

1. Our Responsibility
   a. *Faith apart from works is dead.*—James 2:26 ESV
   b. "After we have offered our petitions, we are to answer them ourselves as far as possible, and not to wait for God to do for us what we can do ourselves. The help of God is held in reserve for all who demand it. Divine help is to be combined with human effort, aspiration, and energy."[29]

Claiming *Bible* promises is not to take the place of other types of praying and worship. It is not a process apart from *Bible* study. Study the context of the promise to make sure that our use of it is warranted.

Foster a spirit of encouragement and rejoicing when we hear others share their experience of answered prayer and use of promises. We are not all at the same stage of spiritual maturity. A judgmental spirit can be discouraging and have a negative effect on another Christian. We should not sit in judgment of another Christian's experience or use of promises. We would do well to enjoy each other as we walk with the Lord and to rejoice in another's experience in the Lord.

PROBLEM OF PRESUMPTION

1. Definition: **Presumption** is the act of taking God's blessings for granted—to act or proceed with unwarrantable or impertinent boldness.

2. Relevance: "**Presumption** is Satan's counterfeit of faith."[30] "A belief that does not lead to obedience is presumption."[31]

HOW TO GUARD AGAINST PRESUMPTION WHEN CLAIMING GOD'S PROMISES

1. **Do not leave any conditions unfulfilled**.

   a. Faith claims God's **promises,** and brings forth fruit in obedience.

   b. **Presumption** also claims the **promises**, but uses them as Satan did, to excuse sin.

   c. Genuine faith has its foundation in the **promises** and provisions of the Scripture.

"There are persons who believe that they are right, when they are wrong. While claiming Christ as their Lord, and professedly doing great works in His name, they are workers of iniquity ... 'Believe, believe,' they say, 'and you need not keep the law.' But a belief that does not lead to obedience is **presumption**. Obedience is the test of discipleship. It is the keeping of the commandments that proves the sincerity of our professions of love ... *And hereby we do know that we know Him, if we keep His commandments.*—1 John 2:3 KJV"[32]

2. **Do not claim that prayer will always be answered in the very way and for the particular thing desired.**

Growing in the "YES" of God

a. "When we do not receive the very things we ask for, at the time we ask, we are still to believe that the Lord hears and that He will answer our prayers. We are so erring and shortsighted that we sometimes ask for things that would not be a blessing to us, and our heavenly Father in love answers our prayer by giving us that which we ourselves would desire if with vision divinely enlightened we could see all things as they really are.

b. When our prayer seems not to be answered, we are to cling to the promise for the time of answering will surely come, and we shall receive the blessing we need most. But to claim that prayer will always be answered in the very way and for the particular thing that we desire is presumption."[33] (Note: the key word is "always.")

PRAYING IN FAITH OR PRESUMPTION

In your own words, what is:

Praying in **Faith**?

_____

_____

_____

_____

Praying in **Presumption**?

_____

_____

_____

_____

What are the dangers of **Praying in Presumption**?

_____

_____

_____

_____

_____

What two ways can **Presumption** sneak up on us?

_____

_____

_____

_____

God's Gift of Assurance

We are invited to call God "our Father."

"In order to strengthen our confidence in God, Christ teaches us to address Him by a new name, a name entwined with the dearest associations of the human heart. He gives us the privilege of calling the infinite God "our Father." This name, spoken to Him and of Him, is a sign of our love and trust toward Him, and a pledge of His regard and relationship to us. Spoken when asking His favor or blessing, it is as music in His ears. That we might not think it **presumption** to call Him by this name, He has repeated it again and again. He desires us to become familiar with the appellation. God regards us as His children."[34]

Growing in the "YES" of God

Review

Let us review our study from Lesson 1 on the vocal conditions:

1. **ASK** For any gift that He has promised we are to **ask**—Matthew 7:7
2. **BELIEVE** Then we are to **believe** that we receive.—Mark 11:24
3. **THANK** And return **thanks** that we have received.—Colossians 4:2. Tell God your needs and don't forget to **thank** Him for His answers.— Philippians 4:6

We can approach God with confidence for this reason; if we make request which accord with His will He listens to us. And if we know that our requests are heard, we know also that the things we ask for are ours.— 1 John 5:14-15 NEB

"Our devotional exercises should not consist wholly in asking and receiving. Let us not be always thinking of our wants and never of the benefits we receive. We do not pray any too much, but we are too sparing of giving thanks. We are the constant recipients of God's mercies, and yet how little gratitude we express, how little we praise Him for what He has done for us."[35]

"Then with self dead, and your life hid with Christ in God, offer your humble petitions."[36]

Assignment

*(If you are working this study in conjunction with **Living Volume One: Praying in the "YES" of God,** you should be reading through page 28.)*

1. Pray the following prayers

   The following **prayers** should be prayed once or twice a day. We want you to establish the habit of daily **asking** for the Holy Spirit to fill you, direct you, and use you. We also want you to remember to intercede in behalf of others. As you establish these habits, you are also incorporating the components of **asking**, **believing**, and **thanking** God into your prayers. **Thank** God immediately, because when you pray, He begins working on the answer. Often those things we **pray** for were put in our heart by Him, because He already has an answer waiting.

There is nothing sacred about these exact words. The suggestions here are just to help you remember the necessity of complying with God's instructions and including these elements as you petition God's blessings.

Daily Prayer Sheet

For Forgiveness

Dear Heavenly Father,

I **ask** that You will forgive me for _____;

I **believe** that You have forgiven me because You have promised in 1 John 1:9;

I **thank** You that You have forgiven me.

In Jesus' name, Amen.

For Intercession and Soul Winning

Dear Heavenly Father,

I **ask** that You will give me life to give _____;

I **believe** that You are giving me life to give him/her because You have promised in 1 John 5:16;

I **thank** You that You have given me life to give him/her.

In Jesus' name, Amen.

For the Holy Spirit

Dear Heavenly Father,

I **ask** that You will give me the Holy Spirit;

I **believe** that You are giving me the Holy Spirit because You have promised in Luke 11:13;

I **thank** You that You have given me the Holy Spirit.

In Jesus' name, Amen.

The Holy Spirit is given without measure to every follower of Christ when the whole heart is surrendered for his indwelling. Jesus says, *Be filled with the Spirit.*—Ephesians 5:18. His command is a promise of its fulfillment.

2. *Bible* Promises for Problems in Everyday Life

   Find five *Bible* **promises** dealing with everyday life problems that you could use for yourself or share with a friend in trouble. A list of *Bible* **Promises** can be found in Appendix A or look at the Concordance at the back of your *Bible*, or in a *Bible* Concordance under the subject of your prayer need.

   It is important to pray the promises set out in God's Word. Using the **Record of Experience** found at the end of this chapter (a blank **Record of Experience** page is located in Appendix A, feel free to make copies as you need), record the Scriptures that God reveals to you and how they apply to the personal problems that you may be having at this time.

   Ask the Holy Spirit to guide your thoughts as you record personal **Prayer Promises** for this week.

3. Read *Privilege of Prayer* on the next page.

4. Journal on the **Reflections** page

   Using your own personal journal or the **Reflections** page found in this chapter or in Appendix A, record how the reading of **Privilege of Prayer** changed you and your approach to life and/or some of the important points that spoke to you from your reading.

   Using your journal or **Reflections** page, what questions or answers did this week's lesson provoke? This is your reflections page. While you are encouraged to share all that God is doing in your life, know that its contents are private, or for you to share as you feel comfortable.

5. In preparation for the next chapter study, please read pages 36-59 in ***Living Volume One: Praying in the "YES" of God***.

The Privilege of Prayer

God speaks to us through nature, the *Bible*, and by the influence of His Spirit. He also speaks through the way He leads us. But it is not enough for Him to speak to us. If we are to have spiritual life and strength, we need to express our desires and our love to Him.

Our minds may be drawn toward Him. We may think of His works, His mercies, and His blessings. But this is not in the fullest sense sharing our thoughts and feelings with Him. We must have something to say to Him about our joys and sorrows, our daily life.

Prayer is the opening of the heart to God as to a friend. Of course we do not need to tell God about ourselves, for He already knows everything. But we pray to help us know Him and be able to receive Him. Prayer does not bring God down to us; it brings us up to Him.

When Jesus was on earth, He taught His disciples how to pray. He told them to present their daily needs before God and to lay all their cares on Him. And He promised that their prayers would be heard. This promise is also for us.

Jesus prayed often. He made Himself one of us when He was on earth. His needs were the same as ours, and He asked His Father for strength to meet the duties of each day. He knew He must have God's help to carry on His work. He is our example in all things.

Jesus shared in our weaknesses, for He was *in all points tempted like as we are.*—Hebrews 4:15 KJV. But He was sinless and turned away from evil. He bore pain and the torture of temptation. Though He was divine, He also was human and needed to pray as we do. He had the right to ask His Father for things He needed. It gave Him comfort and joy to share His thoughts with His Father. The Savior, the Son of God, felt the need of prayer. How much more should we who are weak, sinful people feel the need to turn to God in prayer.

Our heavenly Father waits to give us His full blessing. In prayer we can feel His boundless love. What a wonder it is that we pray so little! God is ready and willing to hear the sincere prayer of even the most humble child, but still we seem almost afraid to tell Him what we need.

Growing in the "YES" of God

What must the angels of heaven think of poor, helpless people who are tempted to sin and yet will not ask for help? God's heart of infinite love is ready to give them more than they can ask or think. Yet they pray so little and have such little faith. The angels love to bow before God; they love to be near Him. Their greatest joy is sharing their time and thoughts with Him. The people of earth need the help that only God can give. Yet they seem willing to live without feeling Him near and without the light of His Spirit.

The darkness of Satan, the evil one, is around those who do not pray. The enemy leads them into sin because they do not meet with God in prayer. Why should the sons and daughters of God be slow to pray? God has a great storehouse of blessings, and prayer is the key in the hand of faith that unlocks heaven's storehouse.

Unless we pray often, we are in danger of growing careless. We may be led to turn from the right path. Satan is always trying to block the path to God. He does not want us to receive grace and power through prayer to resist evil.

We can expect God to answer our prayers, but we must meet certain conditions. One of the first conditions is that we must feel our need of help from Him. He has promised, *I will give water to the thirsty land and make streams flow on the dry ground.*—Isaiah 44:3 GNB. Those who are hungry and thirsty for God's righteousness will be filled. The heart must be open to the Spirit's influence, or His blessings cannot be received.

We need God's help. He knows this and wants to give it to us, but we must ask Him for it. He says, *Ask, and you will receive.*—Matthew 7:7 GNB. Paul wrote that *God ... did not even keep back his own Son, but offered him for us all! He gave us his Son.—will he not also freely give us all things?*—Romans 8:32 GNB.

The Lord will not hear us if we hold on to any known sin. But He always hears the prayers of a person who is sorry for sin. When all known wrongs are made right, we may believe that God will answer our prayers. Our own goodness will never cause God to love us. It is the goodness of Jesus that will save us; it is His blood that will make us clean. Yet we have a work to do in meeting the conditions for being accepted.

We also need faith when we pray. *No one can please God without faith, for whoever comes to God must have faith that God exists and rewards those who seek him.*—Hebrews 11:6 GNB. Jesus said to His disciples, *When you pray and ask for something, believe that you have received it, and you will be given whatever you ask for.*—Mark 11:24 GNB. Do we take Him at His word?

God is faithful in keeping His many promises. We may sometimes ask and not receive at once the things we ask for. But we are still to believe that the Lord hears and that He will answer our prayers.

We cannot see the future, and sometimes we ask for things that would not be a blessing. Our heavenly Father in love answers our prayers by giving us what is best for us. He gives us what we would ask for if we could see all things as they really are.

We are to hold to God's promises even when it seems that our prayers are not answered. At the right time we will receive the blessing we need most. But we cannot demand that a prayer will be answered in just the way we desire. God does not make mistakes. He is so good that He will not keep from us anything that would help us. Do not be afraid to trust Him, even though you may not see an answer at once. Believe His promise, *Ask, and you will receive.*—Matthew 7:7 GNB.

If we think about our doubts and fears, they will grow greater. We need to come to God in faith, feeling helpless, as we really are. We must with humble, trusting faith tell Him what we want, even though He knows all things. He sees everything in creation and keeps it all going. He can and will hear our prayer and let light shine into our hearts.

Through sincere prayer we are brought close to the mind of God. We may have no real proof that He is near, but our Redeemer is bending over us in love and sympathy. We may not feel His touch, but His hand is upon us in love and tender pity.

We must have love and forgiveness in our own hearts when we come to God asking for mercy and blessings. We pray, *Forgive us the wrongs we have done, as we forgive the wrongs that others have done to us.*—Matthew 6:12 GNB. How can we pray this if we have an unforgiving spirit? We must forgive others if we expect our prayers to be heard. We will be forgiven as we forgive.

Faithfulness in prayer has been made a condition of receiving. We must pray always if we want to grow in faith. We are to *pray at all times.*—

Growing in the "YES" of God

Romans 12:12 GNB. Paul wrote, *Be persistent in prayer, and keep alert as you pray, giving thanks to God.*—Colossians 4:2 GNB.

Peter told the believers to be *alert, to be able to pray.*—1 Peter 4:7 GNB. Paul told them, *Don't worry about anything, but in all your prayers ask God for what you need, always asking Him with a thankful heart.*—Philippians 4:6 GNB. Jude said, *"But you, my friends, keep on building yourselves up ... Pray in the power of the Holy Spirit, and keep yourselves in the love of God.*—Jude 20, 21 GNB.

Regular prayer gives us an unbroken hold on God so that life from Him flows into us. Then purity and holiness flow back to God from our lives.

It is important that nothing keeps us from praying. We must keep open the path between us and Jesus. Whenever it is possible, let us be where people are praying. If we really want a close walk with God, we will go to prayer meeting. We will be eager to receive spiritual blessings. We will place ourselves where we can receive the rays of light from heaven.

Families should pray together. But praying by oneself is important. Praying to God alone keeps our spiritual lives alive. It is impossible for a Christian life to be healthy without prayer. Family and public prayer is not enough. A person should open his heart to God alone in a prayer heard by Him only. No other ear is to hear these secret desires.

We are free from other influences when we are alone with God. We can reach out quietly to Him, and a sweet influence will flow from Him who sees in secret. His ear is open to hear our prayer, as with quiet, simple faith we share our thoughts with Him. We receive rays of divine light to help us in the battle with Satan. God is our tower of strength.

We should lift our hearts to God in our homes and as we go about our daily work. This is the way Enoch walked with God. Silent prayers rise to God like smoke from sweet incense. Satan cannot overcome a person who keeps hold of God in prayer.

At any time or any place it is proper to offer a silent prayer to God. Nothing can keep us from lifting our hearts in prayer. We can pray when we are on a crowded street and when we are carrying on our business.

We may pray as did the prophet Nehemiah. While he was standing before the king, he asked God to guide him. Any place we are can be a place of prayer. We can keep the door of the heart open all the time, inviting Jesus in as a heavenly guest.

There may be so much wickedness around us that we feel the air is poisoned, but we may breathe the pure air of heaven. By lifting our hearts to God in prayer we close our minds against thoughts that are not pure and holy. When our hearts are open to receive the blessings of God, our thoughts will be about heavenly things, and we will feel close to God all the time.

We need to understand more clearly why Jesus became a man, and understand better the value of eternal life. The beauty of holiness is to fill the hearts of all Christians. We must ask God to open our eyes that we may better see this beauty.

Our minds should turn to God so that we may breathe the air of heaven. We may keep so near to God that no matter what happens, our thoughts will turn to Him. They will turn as easily as the flower turns to the sun.

We may keep our wants, our joys, our sorrows before God. We may share with Him our cares and fears. We will not make Him weary. He is able to count the hairs of our heads, and He cares about the needs of His children. *For the Lord is full of mercy and compassion.*—James 5:11 GNB.

God's heart of love is touched by our sorrows and even by our telling Him about them. We may take everything that troubles us to Him. Nothing is too great for Him to bear, for He holds up the worlds and rules the universe. Nothing that happens to us is too small for Him to notice. Nothing in our lives is too sinful for Him to know about. No problem is so great He cannot solve it. He shares our joys and our worries. He hears every sincere prayer and is always ready to answer. *He heals the broken-hearted and bandages their wounds.*—Psalm 147:3 GNB. God knows His people perfectly, and He treats each one as though there were not another person for whom He gave His dear Son.

Jesus said, *When that day comes, you will ask him in my name; and I do not say that I will ask him on your behalf, for the Father himself loves you.*—John 16:26-27 GNB. *I chose you ... And so the Father will give you whatever you ask of him in my name.*—John 15:16 GNB. Jesus tells us to pray in His name. But to pray in His name means more than saying His name at the beginning of the prayer and again at the end. It means to pray in the mind and spirit of Jesus. It means that we believe His promises, depend upon His grace, and do His work.

God does not ask us to go away by ourselves and spend all our time praying. We must live a life such as Christ lived. We must work as well as pray. A person who does nothing but pray will soon stop praying, or His prayers will become only a habit.

People who stop helping others and doing their Christian duty have little for which to pray. When they do not work for the Master, who worked for them, they have nothing to pray about. Their prayers are only for themselves. They do not pray for other people or for strength to do God's work.

We lose blessings when we do not meet together to give strength and courage to each other. We begin to forget the truths of God's Word, and they become less important in our minds. Our minds are not touched by the Spirit of God, and we become less spiritual. We lose sympathy for one another when we shut ourselves away from others. We are not then doing what God planned we should do. Being friendly brings us into sympathy with others. It makes us grow and become stronger in the service of God.

We should speak to each other of the love of God and of the plan of salvation. This would bring new life to our hearts and to one another. We would daily learn more about our heavenly Father and receive more of His grace. We would desire to speak of His love, and our own hearts would be warmed and encouraged. We will have more of Christ's presence when we think and talk about Him and not so much about ourselves.

We should delight to talk of God and praise Him. If we would think of Him as often as we are blessed, He would ever be in our thoughts. We talk about our business because this interests us. We talk of our friends because we love them. They are part of our joys and our sorrows. Yet we have a much greater reason to love God than to love our earthly friends. If we make Him first in our thoughts, it will be easy for us to talk of His goodness and tell of His power.

The rich gifts God gives us are not supposed to fill our thoughts until we have no time for Him. They are to keep reminding us of Him and helping us love Him more. Let us look to heaven, where the glory of God shines from the face of Christ. *He is able, now and always, to save those who come to God through him.*—Hebrews 7:25 GNB.

We need to praise God more *for his goodness, and for his wonderful works to the children of men!*—Psalm 107:8 KJV. Our prayers should not be just asking and getting what we asked for. We are not to think always of our wants and never of our blessings. We do not give thanks enough. We are always receiving God's blessings, and yet how little we give thanks! How little we praise Him for what He has done for us!

Long ago the Lord told the people of Israel to meet together at certain times. He said, *There, in the presence of the Lord your God, who has blessed you, you and your families will eat and enjoy the good things that you have worked for.*—Deuteronomy 12:7 GNB. When we do something for the glory of God, we should do it cheerfully, with songs of praise and gladness.

Our God is a kind, merciful Father. Working for Him should be a happy experience. It should be a pleasure to worship the Lord and to take part in His work. God has given us salvation, and He does not want us to think of Him as a hard master. He is our best friend. And when we worship Him, He expects to be with us and bless us. He wants to fill our hearts with joy and love.

The Lord desires us to take comfort in His work. He wants us to find more pleasure than hardship in serving Him. He wants us to carry away happy thoughts of His love and care when we worship Him. These thoughts should bring cheer to our daily work and give us grace to be honest and faithful.

We must make the cross of Christ the center of our lives. We should think and talk about what He did for us. These thoughts should fill us with joy. We should keep in mind the blessings and love we receive from God. We should be willing to trust Jesus with everything, for His hands were nailed to the cross for us.

Praise lifts the heart nearer to heaven. God is worshiped with song and music in heaven, and when we praise God, we worship Him as do the holy angels. He says, *Giving thanks is the sacrifice that honors me.*—Psalm 50:23 GNB. Let us come before our Creator with holy joy. Let us worship Him with *thanksgiving and the voice of melody.*—Isaiah 51:3 KJV [37]

"With what earnestness, then, should we seek God, that He may open our understanding to comprehend the truths brought to us from Heaven."
—*The Sanctified Life*, p. 50

Record of Experiences

Date Asked	Problem	Promise Text	Date Answered	How Answered

Record of Experiences

This record of experiences will help you keep a list of the problems you had, the promises you claimed and the date your prayers were answered. It will help to increase your faith in the future when you can look back and see how God so miraculously intervened.

Speak Lord, Your servant is listening—1 Samuel 3:9-10 NIV

Weekly Reflections

_____

_____

_____

_____

_____

_____

_____

_____

_____

_____

_____

_____

"If you love God and are living for Him, you are probably living out most of the conditions without realizing the importance God places on them or that He names them as conditions."

—*Praying in the "YES" of God, p. 91*

LESSON THREE—CONDITIONS TO ANSWERED PRAYER

Now this is the confidence that we have in Him, that if we ask for anything according to His will, He hears us.
—1 John 5:14

(Please refer to pages 91-95 in **Living Volume One: Praying in the "YES" of God** *while you are studying this chapter.)*

A pastor friend shared the following example, which really struck a cord with me. He said, "Ask someone close to you a favor and maybe 95% of the time they are going to say 'yes.' If 95% of the time they said, 'No,' you wouldn't bother to ask them anymore, would you? It is the same way with God. If His answer is always 'no,' why bother to ask Him?" We are learning how to **Pray in the "YES" of God**, so that the answers are more frequently 'yes.'

God's word was written, not just so we can read and wonder, but so the same power that was manifest in *Bible* times may be made manifest in us today, as in faith we receive all that God desires to impart. We need "to re-

41

gard it (God's word) as it really is—, the Word of the living God, the Word that is our life, the Word that is to mold our actions, our words and our thoughts."[38]

There are certain **conditions** upon which we may expect that God will hear and answer our **prayers—Praying in the "YES" of God**. All promises have the same basic **conditions**. Some promises have extra **conditions** attached to them, which we will study later.

"**Conditions** are really commands, and commands are promises"[39]. All **conditions** are fulfilled in the same way as commands—by claiming them as promises. A command of God, a **condition of God**, becomes a promise of victory to the Christian who relies upon God by faith in Jesus Christ.

As we **pray** the **Prayer of Faith**, "we need look for no outward evidence of blessings. The gift is in the promise, and we may go about our work assured that what God has promised He is able to perform, and that the gift, which we already possess, will be realized when we need it most."[40] *In other words, move forward in faith anticipating the answer, according to God's timing: continue doing your part. After we ask, we proceed, believing that God will establish all that He has promised when we need it most.*

Conditions for Answered Prayer

The following are conditions that need to be incorporated into our **prayer** life when we **Pray in the "YES" of God** presenting the **Prayer of Faith/Reception/Petition**. When we do our part as God has directed we may expect that God will hear and answer our **prayers**.

1. **Need of God**
   (*Reference pages 106-112 in* **Living Volume One: Praying in the "YES" of God**)

   Read **Mark 2:17** and paraphrase it here:

   _____

   Read **Jeremiah 29:13** and paraphrase it here:

   _____

"Jesus loves their souls and He will do a good work for them, if they will humble themselves under His mighty hand, repent and be converted, surrender every day to God. It must be a constant, daily surrender."[41]

2. **Ask in Jesus' Name**
   (*Reference pages 113-117 in **Living Volume One: Praying in the "YES" of God**)

Read John **14:13-14** and paraphrase them here:

_____

_____

Read **John 16:23** and paraphrase it here:

_____

"Ask in My name, Christ says, Make use of My name. This will give your prayers efficacy, and the Father will give you the riches of His grace. Wherefore ask, and ye shall receive that your joy may be full."[42]

"To pray in Christ's name means much. It means that we are to accept His character, manifest His spirit, and work His works. The Savior's promise is given on condition 'If ye love Me, keep my commandments.' He saved men, not in sin but from sin; and those who love Him will show their love by obedience."[43]

"When with earnestness and intensity we breathe a prayer in the name of Christ there is in that very intensity a pledge from God that He is about to answer our prayer *exceeding abundantly above all that we ask or think.*—Ephesians 3:20[44]

It is only because of Jesus sacrificing His life on the cross, and by His atoning blood for sinners like us, that we have access to the Father. Six times our Savior invites us to pray in His Name. When we do, we acknowledge Jesus as our only access/entrance before the Father. We are praying for the accomplishment of His will in behalf of our request.

Growing in the "YES" of God

3. **Perseverance**
(Reference pages 118-125 in Living Volume One: Praying in the "YES" of God)

"When we pray for earthly blessings, the answer to our prayer maybe delayed or God may give us something other than we ask, but not so when we ask for deliverance from sin."[45]

Read **Ephesians 6:18** and paraphrase it here:

_____

Read **Psalm 55:17** and paraphrase it here:

_____

Read **Colossians 4:2** and paraphrase it here:

_____

Definition: Persistence in anything undertaken, continue resolutely. We must pray resolutely if we are to grow in faith and experience.

"**Perseverance** in prayer has been made a condition of receiving. We must pray always if we would grow in faith and experience. We are to be *instant in prayer*, to *continue in prayer*, and watch in the same with thanksgiving.'"—Romans 12:12, Colossians 4:2[46]

4. **Diligence**
   (Reference pages 118-125 in *Living Volume One: Praying in the "YES" of God*)

   Read **1 Thessalonians 5:17** and paraphrase it here:

   _____

   Read **Hebrews 11:6** and paraphrase it here:

   _____

   Read **Colossians 4:2** and paraphrase it here:

   _____

This reminds us of the acronym **PUSH**. **P**ray **U**ntil **S**omething **H**appens! God want us to keep on praying even when we don't see an immediate answer, resting in the assurance that He is working on the answer and that we can trust in His timing.

Definition: **Diligence** is carefulness, steady application.

"There is necessity for **diligence** in prayer; let nothing hinder you. Those who are really seeking for communion with God will be seen in the prayer meetings ... We should pray in the family circle. We must not neglect secret prayer. Pray in your closet, and as you go about your daily labor. There is no time or place in which it is inappropriate to offer up a petition to God."[47]

Note: At first glance, **perseverance** and **diligence** may appear to mean the same thing. Word experts, however, indicate there is a distinct difference. Perseverance indicates nothing about the quality or quantity of the work accomplished, only the unflagging nature of the effort, where diligence suggests the performing of the work that is well done and that demands the worker's alertness and dedication to the task.

5. **Seek First the Kingdom**
   (*Reference pages 126-131 in **Living Volume One: Praying in the "YES" of God**)*

   Read **Matthew 6:33** and paraphrase it here:

   _____

   Jesus, our example, spent time each morning with the Father to prepare for the demands of each day. God provided for Jesus and He will provide for us.

6. **Responsive Heart**   7. **Humility**   8. **Repentance**
   (*Reference pages 132-138 and 75-83 in **Living Volume One: Praying in the "YES" of God**)*

   Read **2 Kings 22:19** and paraphrase it here:

   _____

   Read **2 Chronicles 7:14** and paraphrase it here:

   _____

Jesus provides opportunities for those who are willing. For those who will humble themselves and respond with a true heart of repentance. For those who will listen, Jesus provides answers.

"To Jesus, who emptied Himself for the salvation of lost humanity, the Holy Spirit was given without measure. So it will be given to every follower of Christ when the whole heart is surrendered for His indwelling. Our Lord Himself has given the command, *Be filled with the Spirit.*—Ephesians 5:18, and this command is also a promise of its fulfillment. It was the good pleasure of the Father that in Christ should *all the fullness dwell,* and *in Him ye are made full.*—Colossians 1:19[48]

9. **Obedience**
   *(Reference pages 139-147 in **Living Volume One: Praying in the "YES" of God**)*

   Read **1 John 3:21-22** and paraphrase them here:

   _____

   _____

   "Obedience is the test of discipleship."[49] "We are to give ourselves to Christ, to live a life of willing obedience to all His requirements. All that we are, all the talents and capabilities we possess, are the Lord's to be consecrated to His service. When we thus give ourselves wholly to Him, Christ, with all the treasures of Heaven, gives Himself to us."[50]

   The fulfillment of this condition embraces many of the other conditions. When we walk in obedience, it is because of our faith and our sense of need of God. We are patiently waiting as we diligently seek Him; persevering hopefully because of our love for God and others with a pure heart that has sought and given forgiveness in humility seeking first the Kingdom of God.

10. **Faith**
    *(Reference pages 139-147 in **Living Volume One: Praying in the "YES" of God**)*

    Read **Hebrews 11:6** and paraphrase it here:

    _____

    Read **Romans 12:3** and paraphrase it here:

    _____

Growing in the "YES" of God

Faith lays hold of the promises of God with thanksgiving and patience. "... Man needs a power out of and above himself to restore him to the likeness of God; but because he needs divine aid, it does not make human activity unessential. **Faith** on the part of man is required; for **faith** works by love and purifies the soul. **Faith** lays hold upon the virtue of Christ.[51]

11. **Patience**
    *(Reference pages 139-147 in **Living Volume One: Praying in the "YES" of God**)*

    Read **Hebrews 6:12** and paraphrase it here:

    _____

    Noah responded to God in obedience, faith and patience.

12. **Love**
    *(Reference pages 148-162 in **Living Volume One: Praying in the "YES" of God**)*

    Read **1 John 4:7** and paraphrase it here:

    _____

    Read **Colossians 3:14** and paraphrase it here:

    _____

    Read **John 15:12** and paraphrase it here:

    _____

13. **Forgiveness**
    (Reference pages 148-162 in *Living Volume One: Praying in the "YES" of God*)

    Read **Matthew 6:14-15** and paraphrase them here:

    _____

    _____

    Read **Acts 26:18** and paraphrase it here:

    _____

    Read **1 John 1:9** and paraphrase it here:

    _____

    "When we come to ask mercy and blessing from God we should have a spirit of love and forgiveness in our hearts. How can we pray, *Forgive us our debts, as we forgive our debtors*, and yet indulge an unforgiving spirit?—Matthew 6:12"[52]

    Our prayer will be, "Father, help me to love with Your love and forgive with Your forgiveness."

14. **Concern for Others with Unselfish Motive/Intercession**
    (Reference pages 163-174 in *Living Volume One: Praying in the "YES" of God*)

    Read **1 John 5:16** and paraphrase it here:

    _____

    Read **Isaiah 50:4** and paraphrase it here:

    _____

Read **Ephesians 6:18** and paraphrase it here:

_____

15. **Pure Heart**

Read **Psalm 139:23-24** and paraphrase them here:

_____

To give up **cherished sins,** to let go of them is a condition to answered prayer. We do not want to hold on to anything that would come between God and us. May God reveal anything in our heart that we are unwilling to see.

Reflection Thoughts—Are you holding onto cherished sin? Pray and ask God to reveal them to you. **Ask** forgiveness and **Believe** you are forgiven and **Thank** Him for His forgiveness.

The story of Abraham, the promises realized through faith, is an example for us. Read **Romans 4:13-25** and be encouraged. Look to it for the reassurance that God has a plan and purpose for your life as well as for the saints of yesterday.

"To Jesus, who emptied Himself for the salvation of lost humanity, the Holy Spirit was given without measure. So it will be given to every follower of Christ when the whole heart is surrendered for His indwelling. Our Lord Himself has given the command, "Be filled with the Spirit," and this command is also a promise of its fulfillment."[53]

Assignment

1. Pray the prayers on the **Daily Prayer Sheet**

   For Forgiveness

   Dear Heavenly Father,

   I **ask** that You will forgive me for _____;

   I **believe** that You have forgiven me because You have promised in 1 John 1:9;

   I **thank** You that You have forgiven me.

   In Jesus' name, Amen.

   For Intercession and Soul Winning

   Dear Heavenly Father,

   I **ask** that You will give me life to give _____;

   I **believe** that You are giving me life to give him/her because You have promised in 1 John 5:16;

   I **thank** You that You have given me life to give him/her.

   In Jesus' name, Amen.

   For the Holy Spirit

   Dear Heavenly Father,

   I **ask** that You will give me the Holy Spirit;

   I **believe** that You are giving me the Holy Spirit because You have promised in Luke 11:13;

   I **thank** You that You have given me the Holy Spirit.

   In Jesus' name, Amen.

2. *Bible* Promises for your personal needs

   Using the list found in Appendix A, or through your own study, find five *Bible* **promises** for your personal needs.

   It is important to pray the **promises** set out in God's Word. Using the **Record of Experience** found at the end of this chapter, record the Scriptures that the Holy Spirit reveals to you and how they apply to the personal problems that you may be having at this time; then present them to God for fulfillment. Be prepared to share how God has helped you fulfill the **conditions** to answered **prayer**.

3. Memorize the **General Conditions**

4. Read *Faith and Acceptance* on the following pages.

5. Journal on the **Reflections** page. Using your own personal journal or the **Reflections** page found in this chapter or in Appendix A, record how the reading of Faith and Acceptance changed you and your approach to life and/or some of the important points that spoke to you from your reading.

Using your journal or **Reflections** page, what questions or answers did this week's lesson provoke?

Faith and Acceptance

As God's Holy Spirit brings to life the spiritual powers of your mind, you begin to see how evil and strong sin is. You feel the guilt and sorrow it brings, and you hate it. You feel that sin has separated you from God. Its power has made you a slave. The more you try to escape, the more you know that you cannot help yourself. You see that your life has been filled with selfishness and sin. Your heart is unclean and your desires are not pure. You want to be forgiven, to be clean, to be set free. But what can you do to be one with God and to be like Him?

You need peace—Heaven's forgiveness and peace and love. Money cannot buy that peace. Study will not give it. The mind cannot find it. Being wise will not provide it. You can never hope to receive this peace by your own work and power.

God offers His peace to you as a gift. *It will cost you nothing!*—Isaiah 55:1. It is yours if you will reach out your hands and take it. The Lord says, *You are stained red with sin, but I will wash you as clean as snow. Although your stains are deep red, you will be as white as wool.—Isaiah 1:18. I will give you a new heart and a new mind.—Ezekiel 36:26.*

You have confessed your sins and chosen to put them out of your life. You have decided to give yourself to God. Now go to Him and ask Him to wash away your sins. Ask Him to give you a new heart, a new mind. Then believe that He does this, *because He has promised.* Jesus taught this lesson when He was on the earth. You must believe that you receive the gift God promises and that it is yours.

Jesus healed the sick people who had faith in His power. Healing them made them able to see that He could help them in other ways. It led them to believe in His power to forgive sin. Jesus explained this when He was healing a man who was too sick to get out of his bed. He said, *I will prove to you, then, that the Son of Man has authority on earth to forgive sins.* Jesus then spoke to the sick man, *Get up, pick up your bed, and go home!*— Matthew 9:6.

John, the disciple of Jesus, told us why Christ healed people. He wrote, *These have been written in order that you may believe that Jesus is the Messiah, the Son of God, and that through your faith in him you may have life.—John 20:31.*

Growing in the "YES" of God

Read the *Bible* stories about Jesus healing the sick. From them you can learn something of how to believe in Him for the forgiveness of sins. Turn to the story of the sick man at the pool of Bethesda. The poor man was helpless. He had not walked for 38 years. Yet Jesus said to him, *Get up, pick up your bed, and go home!*

The sick man did not say, "Lord, if You make me well, I will obey Your word." No, he believed Christ's word. He believed he was made well, and that very moment he tried to walk. He *chose* to walk. And he did walk. He acted on the word of Christ, and God gave the power. The man was healed.

Now look at yourself. You are a sinner. You can do nothing to take away your past sins. You cannot change your heart or make yourself holy. But God promises to do all this for you through Christ. *Believe* that promise. Confess your sins and give yourself to God. *Choose* to serve Him. God will surely keep His promise to you if you do this. When you believe, God acts. You will be made clean and whole, just as Christ gave the sick man power to walk when he believed that he was healed. It *is* so if you believe it.

Do not wait to *feel* that you are made whole. Say, "I believe it. It *is* so, not because I feel it, but because God has promised."

Jesus said, *When you pray and ask for something, believe that you have received it, and you will be given whatever you ask for.*—Mark 11:24. There is something important to remember in this promise. You must pray for those things that God wants you to have. God wants to free you from sin and make you His child. He wants to give you power to live a holy life.

You may pray for these blessings and believe that you receive them. Then you may thank God that you *have* received them. You may go to Jesus and be made clean and stand before God's law without shame or sadness. *There is no condemnation now for those who live in union with Christ Jesus.*—Romans 8:1.

When you belong to Christ, you are not your own, for you are bought with a price. *God paid a ransom to save you ..., and the ransom he paid was not mere gold or silver ... But he paid for you with the priceless lifeblood of Christ, the sinless, spotless Lamb of God.*—1 Peter 1:18-19 TLB. Because you believe what God has said, the Holy Spirit creates a new life in your heart. You are as a child born into the family of God, and He loves you as He loves His own Son.

Now that you have given yourself to Jesus, do not turn back. Do not take yourself away from Him. Day after day say, "I am Christ's. I have given myself to Him." Ask Him to give you His Spirit and keep you by His grace. You became His child by giving yourself to God and believing in Him. You are to live in Him in the same way. The apostle Paul wrote, *Since you have accepted Christ Jesus as Lord, live in union with him.*—Colossians 2:6.

Some people feel that they are on trial and must prove to the Lord that they have changed before they can receive His blessing. But they may receive the blessing right now. They must have His grace, the Spirit of Christ, to help them overcome their weaknesses. Without it they cannot fight against sin.

Jesus loves to have us come to Him just as we are, sinful, helpless, and needy. We may come, foolish and weak as we are, and fall at His feet in sorrow for sin. It is His glory to put His arms of love around us, heal our wounds, and make us clean.

Thousands believe that Jesus pardons other people, but not them. They do not believe what God says. But every person who truly repents can know for himself that God freely pardons every one of his sins.

Do not fear. God's promises are meant for you. They are for every person who is sorry for his sins. Christ sends angels to bring strength and grace to every believing person. Even the most sinful persons can be strong, pure, and righteous by accepting Jesus, who died for them. Christ is waiting to take away our sin-soiled clothes, and to put on us the clean, white clothes of righteousness. He wants us to live and not die.

God does not treat us the way people treat each other. He thinks of us with love, mercy, and pity. He says, *Let the wicked leave their way of life and change their way of thinking. Let them turn to the Lord, our God; for he is merciful and quick to forgive.*—Isaiah 55:7. *I have swept your sins away like a cloud. Come back to me: I am the one who saves you.*—Isaiah 44:22.

The Lord says, "*do not want anyone to die ... Turn away from your sins and live.*—Ezekiel 18:32. Satan tries to keep you from believing the blessed promises of God. He wants to take away from you every bit of hope and every ray of light. But you must not let him do this. Do not listen to Satan. Say to him, "Jesus died so that I could live. He loves me and does not want me to die. I have a loving heavenly Father. Even though I have turned from His love and wasted His blessings, I will go to my Father. I will say, 'I have sinned against Heaven and against You. I am no longer worthy to be called Your son. Treat me as one of Your hired workers.'"

Jesus told the story of a son who had left home and how he was received when he decided to come back. *He was still a long way from home when his father saw him; his heart was filled with pity, and he ran, threw his arms around his son, and kissed him.*—Luke 15:20.

This is a beautiful story, but it cannot fully tell of the heavenly Father's love and pity. The Lord said through His prophet, *I have always loved you, so I continue to show you my constant love.*—Jeremiah 31:3. The Father is hoping for the sinner's return even while the sinner is far away wasting his life and money in a strange country. When a person feels a desire to return to God, this is God's Spirit calling, trying to bring the sinner to the Father's heart of love.

With the wonderful promises of the *Bible* before you, how can you doubt? How can you think that Jesus will not welcome the sinner who wants to turn from his sins? Put away such thoughts! Nothing can hurt you more than believing such an idea about our heavenly Father.

The Father hates sin, but He loves the sinner. He gave Himself when He gave Christ that all who would believe might be saved. He wanted them to be blessed forever in His kingdom of glory.

What stronger or more loving words could He use to tell us how much He loves us? He said, *Can a woman forget her own baby and not love the child she bore? Even if a mother should forget her child, I will never forget you.*—Isaiah 49:15.

Look up to Jesus if you have doubts and fears. He lives to ask God to forgive your sins. Thank God for the gift of His dear Son. Pray that His death for you will not be useless. The Spirit invites you today. Come with your whole heart to Jesus and receive His blessing.

Read His promises. Remember that they tell of His love and pity, which are stronger than words can tell. God's great heart of infinite love turns to the sinner with never-ending pity. *By the blood of Christ we are set free, that is, our sins are forgiven.*—Ephesians 1:7.

Believe that God is your helper. He wants to change your life, to make it like His perfect life. Come close to Him as you confess your sins and repent, and He will come close to you with mercy and forgiveness."[54]

Record of Experiences

Date Asked	Problem	Promise Text	Date Answered	How Answered

Record of Experiences

This record of experiences will help you keep a list of the problems you had, the promises you claimed and the date your prayers were answered. It will help to increase your faith in the future when you can look back and see how God so miraculously intervened.

Speak Lord, Your servant is listening—1 Samuel 3:9-10 NIV

Weekly Reflections

_____

_____

_____

_____

_____

_____

_____

_____

_____

_____

_____

"God regards us as His children. He has redeemed us out of the careless world and has chosen us to become members of the royal family, sons and daughters of the heavenly King."

—*Christ's Object Lesson,* p. 142

LESSON FOUR—SPIRITUAL LIVING

Oh, worship the Lord in the beauty of holiness
—Psalm 96:9

Introduction

We have studied so far:

1. The three vocal **conditions** to answered prayer.
2. Gospel principles regarding **conditions**.
3. The fourteen general **conditions** to answered prayer.

In this lesson we will study:

1. A special **condition** for claiming God's promises.
2. A recommended procedure for presenting *Bible* promises to God
3. Our responsibility as we claim God's promises
4. Devotional Ideas

59

Growing in the "YES" of God

Besides the **conditions** we have already studied, additional specific **conditions** often occur within the context of a particular **promise**. These also must be fulfilled. Examples will be introduced.

Special Conditions
(Reference page 93 in Living Volume One: Praying in the "YES" of God)

1. **Fulfill any additional conditions attached to a particular promise.**
   a. The conditions studied so far are all we need for many promises; they have no additional conditions in their context.

   Examples:

   Read **Luke 11:13** and paraphrase it here: _____

   _____

   Read **Philippians 4:19** and paraphrase it here: _____

   _____

   b. Additional specific **conditions** often occur within the context of a particular promise. These also must be fulfilled. **Underline or highlight the specific condition in the following examples**:

   If we confess our sins, He is faithful and just to forgive us our sins and to cleanse us from all unrighteousness.—1 John 1:9.

   Thou (God) *dost keep him in perfect peace, whose mind is stayed on thee, because he trusts in thee.*—Isaiah 26:3 RSV.

   Rejoice in the Lord always; ... Let all men know your forbearance ... Have no anxiety about anything, ... and the peace of God, which passes all understanding, will keep your hearts and minds in Christ Jesus.—Philippians. 4:4-7 RSV.

   If any of you lacks wisdom, let him ask God ... with no doubting ...—James 1:5-6.

Count it all joy, my brethren, when you meet various trials, for you know that the testing of your faith produces steadfastness.—James 1:2-3 RSV.

2. **Fulfilling conditions is not accomplished through our power. It can only be done in our faith relationship with Christ. God's biddings are His enablings.**

A Recommended Procedure for Presenting Bible Promises to God

1. "With your *Bible* in your hands say, I have done as You have said, 'I present Your **promises**.' *Ask and it shall be given you; seek, and you shall find; knock, and it shall be opened unto you.*—Matthew 7:7 KJV"[55]

2. "There are many who long to help others, but they feel that they have no spiritual strength or light to impart. Let them present their petitions at the throne of grace. Plead for the Holy Spirit. God stands back of every **promise** He has made"[56] God is the great "Promisor." He is covenanting with us, on His Word. He will fill His part of the covenant **promise**. We must also fill our part. But we do not do that alone. We do it with His assistance."

3. God is anxious to speak to us, to reveal Himself to us, and to reassure us that He hears us. When we pray the **Prayer of Faith**, coming to Him with our *Bible* in our hands, our eyes open searching for the applicable scripture promise, we not only are reassured that we are **Praying in the "YES" of God**, but we give God the opportunity to speak to us through His written word as we open it before Him. In so doing we learn to **Grow in the "YES" of God**.

Our Responsibility

1. *... [F]aith apart from works is dead.*—James 2:26 RSV

2. "After we have offered our petitions, we are to answer them ourselves as far as possible, and not to wait for God to do for us what we can do ourselves. The help of God is held in reserve for all who demand it. Divine help is to be combined with human effort, aspiration, and energy."[57]

3. As we claim **promises** we should study the context of the scripture to make sure that our use of it is warranted.

4. We should not make claiming **promises** a process apart from *Bible* study. This type of praying is to compliment our other communication and study with the Savior.

5. Receive a change of attitude and action through God's power.

   Read **Ezekiel 36:26-27** and paraphrase them here: _____

   _____

6. We are not to sit in judgment on another Christian's experience or use of **promises**. Try to foster a spirit of encouragement and rejoicing when we hear the experience of another person. There are very few Christians who are all at the same stage of maturity and a judgmental spirit can be very negative in its effect on another Christian. Let's learn to enjoy each other as we walk with the Lord and to rejoice in another's experience in the Lord.

   "The long exciting day was past, and Jesus sought rest. But while the city was still wrapped in slumber, the Savior, *rising up a great while before day, ... went out, and departed into a solitary place, and there prayed.*—Mark 1:35 KJV.[58]

Devotional Ideas

1. **Guideline for Being in God's Presence (Karen Cress)**

   a. Let the Lord awaken you each morning.

   b. Remember the purpose is to have a relationship, not just a procedure.

   c. Allow the Holy Spirit to guide you in your devotions.

   d. Keep a journal. Write verses in red and personal comments in blue. (optional)

   e. Have a regular time and place for study.

2. *Four Ways to Make Jesus First in Your Life* **(Ann Ortland)**

   a. Practice His presence by a deliberate act of your will.

   b. Continually withdraw to be with the Father.

   c. Learn to truly worship the Lord.

   d. Always tell Him "YES". Always surrender to His will.

3. **Keep a Journal using "ACTS" (Ann Ortland)**

> **A**—Adoration
> **C**—Confession
> **T**—Thanksgiving
> **S**—Supplication

4. ***Bible* Study Suggestions (source unknown)**

   a. **P**—Prayer for reading
   O—Overview of reading—with description
   S—Scripture text personalized

   M—Meaning (What the verse means to me)
   A—Application to my life
   P—Prayer of application, commitment and prayer needs
   S—Share verse and meaning

   b. Richard Warren's **SPACE PETS**—Choose your *bible* reading, then journal:

   S – Sin to Confess—Do I need to make any restitution?
   P – Promise to claim—Have I met the conditions?
   A – Attitude change—Am I willing to change my attitude?
   C – Command to obey—Am I willing, no matter how I feel?
   E – Example to follow—Is it positive for me to follow or negative to avoid?

   P – Prayer to pray—Anything I need to pray back to God?
   E – Error to avoid—Problem I should be alert to or aware of.
   T – Truth to believe—What new things can I learn about God the Father, Jesus Christ, Holy Spirit, or other biblical teachings?
   S – Something to praise God for—Thankfulness.

   c. Write in journal

   i. Choose a verse from scripture

   ii. Paraphrase it

   iii. Apply verse to experience or plans for the day

   iv. Praise to Him

   v. Prayer of Commitment

d. Treat God's word as written personally—interject your name

e. Do text comparisons

f. Word Studies

g. Chapter summary or analysis

h. Topical Studies

i. Character Qualities

j. Study by Book

k. Biographical

l. Reflection of "yesterday" in prayer and your journal

    i. People you met with

    ii. Decisions you made

    iii. Thoughts or feelings you had

    iv. High Points

    v. Low Points

    vi. Frustrations

    vii. *Bible* reading

    viii. Analyze decisions—good or bad

    ix. Time used, wisely or wasted

    x. What should you have done differently?

    xi. Did you listen to God? Did you hear Him?

5. **Sing Praises to the Lord**

God inhabits the praises of His people and praise dispels the enemy.

6. **Prayer Focus**

Jesus studied the word of God. "He turned aside from the scene of His labor, to go into the fields, to meditate in the green valleys, to hold communion with God on the mountainside or amid the trees of the forest. The early morning often found Him in some secluded place, editing, searching the scriptures, or in prayer. From these quiet hours, He would return to His home to take up His duties again ..."[59] When Jesus' disciples asked Him how to pray, He taught them what we now refer to as the "Lord's Prayer," "Our Father."

Lord's Prayer

from Derek Morris (based upon Matthew 6:9-13)

Focus Upon God

1. Our Father who art in Heaven, hallowed be Your Name
   a. Praise God for His character
   b. Praise God for His works
2. Your Kingdom Come (acceptance of Christ as Savior and Lord)
   a. In my own life
   b. Intercede for others (Family, friends, church, community, world)
3. Your will be done on earth as it is in Heaven
   a. Lay out my plans before the Lord
   b. Accept His agenda

Present Our Need

1. Give us this day our daily bread
   a. Present specific physical needs before the Lord
   b. Claim His promises for provision
2. Forgive us our debts/trespasses as we forgive our debtors/those who trespass against us.
   a. Confess specific personal sins and sins of family
   b. Claim His promises of forgiveness, cleansing and healing
3. And lead us not into temptation but deliver us from evil.
   a. Accept power from God through the anointing of the Holy Spirit
   b. Put on the whole armor of God

Focus upon God

1. For Thine is the Kingdom, and the power and the glory forever.
   a. Conclude by giving praise and glory to God
   b. Trust in His abiding presence. Amen.

Jesus presents His own ideal of prayer, words so simple a child can comprehend them, yet so comprehensive that their significance can never be fully grasped by the greatest minds. We are taught to come to God in praise and thanksgiving, making our requests before the throne of grace in accordance with His promises.

Assignment

1. Pray the prayers on the **Daily Prayer Sheet**

   ### For Forgiveness

   Dear Heavenly Father,

   I **ask** that You will forgive me for _____ ;

   I **believe** that You have forgiven me because You have promised in 1 John 1:9;

   I **thank** You that You have forgiven me.

   In Jesus' name, Amen.

   ### For Intercession and Soul Winning

   Dear Heavenly Father,

   I **ask** that You will give me life to give _____ ;

   I **believe** that You are giving me life to give him/her because You have promised in 1 John 5:16;

   I **thank** You that You have given me life to give him/her.

   In Jesus' name, Amen.

   ### For the Holy Spirit

   Dear Heavenly Father,

   I **ask** that You will give me the Holy Spirit;

   I **believe** that You are giving me the Holy Spirit because You have promised in Luke 11:13;

   I **thank** You that You have given me the Holy Spirit.

   In Jesus' name, Amen.

2. *Bible* Promises for your personal needs

   It is important to pray the promises set out in God's Word. Using the **Record of Experiences**, record the Scriptures that the Holy Spirit reveals to you and how they apply to the personal problems that you may be having at this time, then present them to God for fulfillment.

3. Record five *Bible* promises with the conditions underlined in red and the gifts underlined in blue.

4. Memorize the vocal and general conditions.

5. Read *Asking to Give* on the following pages

6. Journal on the **Reflections** page

Using your own personal journal or the **Reflections** page found in this chapter or in Appendix A, record how the reading of *Asking to Give* changed you and your approach to life and/or some of the important points that spoke to you from your reading.

Using your journal or **Reflections** page, what questions or answers did this week's lesson provoke?

Asking to Give

Christ was continually receiving from the Father that He might communicate to us. *The word which ye hear,* He said, *is not Mine, but the Father's which sent Me.*—John 14:24 KJV. *The Son of man came not to be ministered unto, but to minister.*—Matthew 20:28 KJV. Not for Himself, but for others, He lived and thought and prayed. From hours spent with God He came forth morning by morning, to bring the light of heaven to men. Daily He received a fresh baptism of the Holy Spirit. In the early hours of the new day the Lord awakened Him from His slumbers, and His soul and His lips were anointed with grace, that He might impart to others. His words were given Him fresh from the heavenly courts, words that He might speak in season to the weary and oppressed. *The Lord God hath given Me,* He said, *the tongue of the learned, that I should know how to speak a word in season to him that is weary: He wakeneth morning by morning, He wakeneth Mine ear to hear as the learned.*—Isaiah 50:4 KJV.

Christ's disciples were much impressed by His prayers and by His habit of communion with God. One day after a short absence from their Lord, they found Him absorbed in supplication. Seeming unconscious of their presence, He continued praying aloud. The hearts of the disciples were deeply moved. As He ceased praying, they exclaimed, "Lord, teach us to pray."

In answer, Christ repeated the Lord's Prayer, as He had given it in the sermon on the mount. Then in a parable He illustrated the lesson He desired to teach them.

"Which of you," He said, "shall have a friend, and shall go unto him at midnight, and say unto him, Friend, lend me three loaves; for a friend of mine in his journey is come to me, and I have nothing to set before him? And he from within shall answer and say, Trouble me not; the door is now shut, and my children are with me in bed: I cannot rise and give thee. I say unto you, Though he will not rise and give him because he is his friend, yet because of his importunity he will rise and give him as many as he needeth."

Here Christ represents the petitioner as asking that he may give again. He must obtain the bread, else he cannot supply the necessities of a weary, belated wayfarer. Though his neighbor is unwilling to be troubled, he will not desist his pleading; his friend must be relieved; and at last his importunity is rewarded, his wants are supplied.

In like manner the disciples were to seek blessings from God. In the feeding of the multitude and in the sermon on the bread from heaven, Christ had opened to them their work as His representatives. They were to give the bread of life to the people. He who had appointed their work, saw how often their faith would be tried. Often they would be thrown into unexpected positions, and would realize their human insufficiency. Souls that were hungering for the bread of life would come to them, and they would feel themselves to be destitute and helpless. They must receive spiritual food, or they would have nothing to impart. But they were not to turn one soul away unfed. Christ directs them to the source of supply. The man whose friend came to him for entertainment, even at the unseasonable hour of midnight, did not turn him away. He had nothing to set before him, but he went to one who had food and pressed his request until the neighbor supplied his need. And would not God, who had sent His servants to feed the hungry, supply their need for His own work?

But the selfish neighbor in the parable does not represent the character of God. The lesson is drawn, not by comparison, but by contrast. A selfish man will grant an urgent request, in order to rid himself of one who disturbs his rest. But God delights to give. He is full of compassion, and He longs to grant the requests of those who come unto Him in faith. He gives to us that we may minister to others and thus become like Himself.

Christ declares, *Ask, and it shall be given you; seek, and ye shall find; knock, and it shall be opened unto you. For every one that asketh receiveth; and he that seeketh findeth; and to him that knocketh it shall be opened.—* Matthew 7:7 KJV.

The Savior continues: *If a son shall ask bread of any of you that is a father, will he give him a stone? or if he ask a fish, will he for a fish give him a serpent? or if he shall ask an egg, will he offer him a scorpion? If ye then, being evil, know how to give good gifts unto your children, how much more shall your heavenly Father give the Holy Spirit to them that ask Him?*

In order to strengthen our confidence in God, Christ teaches us to address Him by a new name, a name entwined with the dearest associations of the human heart. He gives us the privilege of calling the infinite God our Father. This name, spoken to Him and of Him, is a sign of our love and trust toward Him, and a pledge of His regard and relationship to us. Spoken when asking His favor or blessing, it is as music in His ears. That we might not think it presumption to call Him by this name, He has repeated it again and again. He desires us to become familiar with the appellation.

Growing in the "YES" of God

God regards us as His children. He has redeemed us out of the careless world and has chosen us to become members of the royal family, sons and daughters of the heavenly King. He invites us to trust in Him with a trust deeper and stronger than that of a child in his earthly father. Parents love their children, but the love of God is larger, broader, deeper, than human love can possibly be. It is immeasurable. Then if earthly parents know how to give good gifts to their children, how much more shall our Father in heaven give the Holy Spirit to those who ask Him?

Christ's lessons in regard to prayer should be carefully considered. There is a divine science in prayer, and His illustration brings to view principles that all need to understand. He shows what is the true spirit of prayer, He teaches the necessity of perseverance in presenting our requests to God, and assures us of His willingness to hear and answer prayer.

Our prayers are not to be a selfish asking, merely for our own benefit. We are to ask that we may give. The principle of Christ's life must be the principle of our lives. "For their sakes," He said, speaking of His disciples, "I sanctify Myself, that they also might be sanctified." John 17:19. The same devotion, the same self-sacrifice, the same subjection to the claims of the word of God, that were manifest in Christ, must be seen in His servants. Our mission to the world is not to serve or please ourselves; we are to glorify God by co-operating with Him to save sinners. We are to ask blessings from God that we may communicate to others. The capacity for receiving is preserved only by imparting. We cannot continue to receive heavenly treasure without communicating to those around us.

In the parable the petitioner was again and again repulsed, but he did not relinquish his purpose. So our prayers do not always seem to receive an immediate answer; but Christ teaches that we should not cease to pray. Prayer is not to work any change in God; it is to bring us into harmony with God. When we make request of Him, He may see that it is necessary for us to search our hearts and repent of sin. Therefore He takes us through test and trial, He brings us through humiliation, that we may see what hinders the working of His Holy Spirit through us.

There are conditions to the fulfillment of God's promises, and prayer can never take the place of duty. *If ye love Me*, Christ says, *Keep My commandments. He that hath My commandments, and keepeth them, he it is that loveth Me; and he that loveth Me shall be loved of My Father, and I will love him, and will manifest Myself to him.*—John 14:15, 21 KJV. Those who bring their petitions to God, claiming His promise while they do not comply with the conditions, insult Jehovah. They bring the name of Christ as their authority for the fulfillment of the promise, but they do not those things that would show faith in Christ and love for Him.

Many are forfeiting the condition of acceptance with the Father. We need to examine closely the deed of trust wherewith we approach God. If we are disobedient, we bring to the Lord a note to be cashed when we have not fulfilled the conditions that would make it payable to us. We present to God His promises, and ask Him to fulfill them, when by so doing He would dishonor His own name.

The promise is *If ye abide in Me, and My words abide in you, ye shall ask what ye will, and it shall be done unto you.*—John 15:7 KJV. And John declares: *And hereby we do know that we know him, if we keep his commandments. He that saith, I know him, and keepeth not his commandments, is a liar, and the truth is not in him. But whoso keepeth his word, in him verily is the love of God perfected: hereby know we that we are in him.*—1 John 2:3-5 KJV.

One of Christ's last commands to His disciples was *Love one another as I have loved you.*—John 13:34. Do we obey this command, or are we indulging sharp, un-Christlike traits of character? If we have in any way grieved or wounded others, it is our duty to confess our fault and seek for reconciliation. This is an essential preparation that we may come before God in faith, to ask His blessing.

There is another matter too often neglected by those who seek the Lord in prayer. Have you been honest with God? By the prophet Malachi the Lord declares, *Even from the days of your fathers ye are gone away from mine ordinances, and have not kept them. Return unto me, and I will return unto you, saith the LORD of hosts. But ye said, Wherein shall we return? Will a man rob God? Yet ye have robbed me. But ye say, Wherein have we robbed thee? In tithes and offerings.*—Malachi 3:7-8 KJV.

As the Giver of every blessing, God claims a certain portion of all we possess. This is His provision to sustain the preaching of the gospel. And by making this return to God, we are to show our appreciation of His gifts. But if we withhold from Him that which is His own, how can we claim His blessing? If we are unfaithful stewards of earthly things, how can we expect Him to entrust us with the things of heaven? It may be that here is the secret of unanswered prayer.

Growing in the "YES" of God

But the Lord in His great mercy is ready to forgive, and He says, *Bring ye all the tithes into the storehouse, that there may be meat in mine house, and prove me now herewith, ... if I will not open you the windows of heaven, and pour you out a blessing, that there shall not be room enough to receive it. And I will rebuke the devourer for your sakes, and he shall not destroy the fruits of your ground; neither shall your vine cast her fruit before the time in the field ... And all nations shall call you blessed; for ye shall be a delightsome land, saith the LORD of hosts.*—Malachi 3:10-12 KJV.

So it is with every other one of God's requirements. All His gifts are promised on condition of obedience. God has a heaven full of blessings for those who will co-operate with Him. All who obey Him may with confidence claim the fulfillment of His promises

But we must show a firm, undeviating trust in God. Often He delays to answer us in order to try our faith or test the genuineness of our desire. Having asked according to His word, we should believe His promise and press our petitions with a determination that will not be denied

God does not say, Ask once, and you shall receive. He bids us ask. Unwearyingly persist in prayer. The persistent asking brings the petitioner into a more earnest attitude, and gives him an increased desire to receive the things for which he asks. Christ said to Martha at the grave of Lazarus, *If thou wouldest believe, thou shouldest see the glory of God.*—John 11:40 KJV.

But many have not a living faith. This is why they do not see more of the power of God. Their weakness is the result of their unbelief. They have more faith in their own working than in the working of God for them. They take themselves into their own keeping. They plan and devise, but pray little, and have little real trust in God. They think they have faith, but it is only the impulse of the moment. Failing to realize their own need, or God's willingness to give, they do not persevere in keeping their requests before the Lord.

Our prayers are to be as earnest and persistent as was the petition of the needy friend who asked for the loaves at midnight. The more earnestly and steadfastly we ask, the closer will be our spiritual union with Christ. We shall receive increased blessings because we have increased faith.

Our part is to pray and believe. Watch unto prayer. Watch, and co-operate with the prayer-hearing God. Bear in mind that *we are laborers together with God.*—1 Corinthians 3:9 KJV. Speak and act in harmony with your prayers. It will make an infinite difference with you whether trial shall prove your faith to be genuine, or show that your prayers are only a form.

When perplexities arise, and difficulties confront you, look not for help to humanity. Trust all with God. The practice of telling our difficulties to others only makes us weak, and brings no strength to them. It lays upon them the burden of our spiritual infirmities, which they cannot relieve. We seek the strength of erring, finite man, when we might have the strength of the unerring, infinite God.

You need not go to the ends of the earth for wisdom, for God is near. It is not the capabilities you now possess or ever will have that will give you success. It is that which the Lord can do for you. We need to have far less confidence in what man can do and far more confidence in what God can do for every believing soul. He longs to have you reach after Him by faith. He longs to have you expect great things from Him. He longs to give you understanding in temporal as well as in spiritual matters. He can sharpen the intellect. He can give tact and skill. Put your talents into the work, ask God for wisdom, and it will be given you.

Take the word of Christ as your assurance. Has He not invited you to come unto Him? Never allow yourself to talk in a hopeless, discouraged way. If you do you will lose much. By looking at appearances and complaining when difficulties and pressure come, you give evidence of a sickly, enfeebled faith. Talk and act as if your faith was invincible. The Lord is rich in resources; He owns the world. Look heavenward in faith. Look to Him who has light and power and efficiency.

There is in genuine faith a buoyancy, a steadfastness of principle, and a fixedness of purpose that neither time nor toil can weaken. *Even the youths shall faint and be weary, and the young men shall utterly fall: but they that wait upon the Lord shall renew their strength; they shall mount up with wings as eagles; they shall run, and not be weary; and they shall walk, and not faint.*—Isaiah 40:30-31 KJV.

There are many who long to help others, but they feel that they have no spiritual strength or light to impart. Let them present their petitions at the throne of grace. Plead for the Holy Spirit. God stands back of every promise He has made. With your *Bible* in your hands say, I have done as Thou hast said. I present Thy promise, *Ask, and it shall be given you; seek, and ye shall find; knock, and it shall be opened unto you.*

Growing in the "YES" of God

We must not only pray in Christ's name, but by the inspiration of the Holy Spirit. This explains what is meant when it is said that the Spirit *maketh intercession for us, with groanings which cannot be uttered.*—Romans 8:26 KJV. Such prayer God delights to answer. When with earnestness and intensity we breathe a prayer in the name of Christ, there is in that very intensity a pledge from God that He is about to answer our prayer *exceeding abundantly above all that we ask or think.*—Ephesians 3:20.

Christ has said, *What things soever ye desire, when ye pray, believe that ye receive them, and ye shall have them.*—Mark 11:24 KJV. *"Whatsoever ye shall ask in My name, that will I do, that the Father may be glorified in the Son.*—John 14:13 KJV. And the beloved John, under the inspiration of the Holy Spirit, speaks with great plainness and assurance: *If we ask anything according to His will, He heareth us: and if we know that He hear us, whatsoever we ask, we know that we have the petitions that we desired of Him.*—1 John 5:14-15. Then press your petition to the Father in the name of Jesus. God will honor that name.

The rainbow round about the throne is an assurance that God is true, that in Him is no variableness, neither shadow of turning. We have sinned against Him, and are undeserving of His favor; yet He Himself has put into our lips that most wonderful of pleas, *Do not abhor us, for thy name's sake; do not disgrace the throne of Thy glory; remember, break not Thy covenant with us.*—Jeremiah 14:21. When we come to him confessing our unworthiness and sin, He has pledged Himself to give heed to our cry. The honor of His throne is staked for the fulfillment of His word unto us.

Like Aaron, who symbolized Christ, our Savior bears the names of all His people on His heart in the holy place. Our great High Priest remembers all the words by which He has encouraged us to trust. He is ever mindful of His covenant.

All who seek of Him shall find. All who knock will have the door opened to them. The excuse will not be made, Trouble Me not; the door is closed; I do not wish to open it. Never will one be told, I cannot help you. Those who beg at midnight for loaves to feed the hungry souls will be successful.

In the parable, he who asks bread for the stranger, receives *as many as he needeth.* And in what measure will God impart to us that we may impart to others? *According to the measure of the gift of Christ.*—Ephesians 4:7 KJV. Angels are watching with intense interest to see how man is dealing with his fellow men. When they see one manifest Christ-like sympathy for the erring, they press to his side and bring to his remembrance words to speak that will be as the bread of life to the soul. So "God shall supply all your need according to His riches in glory by Christ Jesus." Philippians 4:19. Your testimony in its genuineness and reality He will make powerful in the power of the life to come. The word of the Lord will be in your mouth as truth and righteousness.

Personal effort for others should be preceded by much secret prayer; for it requires great wisdom to understand the science of saving souls. Before communicating with men, commune with Christ. At the throne of heavenly grace obtain a preparation for ministering to the people.

Let your heart break for the longing it has for God, for the living God. The life of Christ has shown what humanity can do by being partaker of the divine nature. All that Christ received from God we too may have. Then ask and receive. With the persevering faith of Jacob, with the unyielding persistence of Elijah, claim for yourself all that God has promised.

Let the glorious conceptions of God possess your mind. Let your life be knit by hidden links to the life of Jesus. He who commanded the light to shine out of darkness is willing to shine in your heart, to give the light of the knowledge of the glory of God in the face of Jesus Christ. The Holy Spirit will take the things of God and show them unto you, conveying them as a living power into the obedient heart. Christ will lead you to the threshold of the Infinite. You may behold the glory beyond the veil, and reveal to men the sufficiency of Him who ever liveth to make intercession for us.[60]

"The resounding evidence of the Holy Spirit in a person's life is the unmistakable family likeness to Jesus Christ, and the freedom from everything which is not like Him."
—Oswald Chambers,
My Utmost for His Highest, February 8

Record of Experiences

This record of experiences will help you keep a list of the problems you had, the promises you claimed and the date your prayers were answered. It will help to increase your faith in the future when you can look back and see how God so miraculously intervened.

Date Asked	Problem	Promise Text	Date Answered	How Answered

Speak Lord, Your servant is listening—1 Samuel 3:9-10 NIV

Weekly Reflections

_____

_____

_____

_____

_____

_____

_____

_____

_____

_____

_____

_____

"From the Cross of Calvary, Christ calls for an unconditional surrender."

—*4 Testimonies*, p. 120

LESSON FIVE—HINDRANCES TO ANSWERED PRAYER

Then they will call upon Me, but I will not answer; they will seek Me diligently but will not find Me.

—Proverbs 1:28 ESV

*(Please refer to pages 195-203 in **Living Volume One: Praying in the "YES" of God** while you are studying this chapter.)*

"To have the religion of Christ means that you have absolutely surrendered your all to God, and consented to the guidance of the Holy Spirit. Through the gift of the Holy Spirit, moral power will be given you, and not only will you have your former entrusted talents for the service of God, but their efficiency will be greatly multiplied. The surrender of all our powers to God greatly simplifies the problem of life. It weakens and cuts short a thousand struggles with the passions of the natural heart."[61]

Introduction

We have studied so far:

1. Objective and benefits of this course
2. Prayer of Faith
   a. Types of Prayer
   b. The three vocal conditions to answered prayers.
3. Fundamental gospel principles regarding conditions.
   a. Presumption
   b. God's gift of assurance
4. The fifteen general conditions to answered prayer.
5. Spiritual Living
   a. Special condition for claiming God's promises.
   b. A recommended procedure for presenting *Bible* promises to God.
   c. Our responsibility as we claim God's promises.
   d. Devotional Ideas.

In this lesson we will look at:

1. Causes of failure in our prayers being answered.
2. The hindrances to answered prayer.

Causes of Failure of Our Prayers Being Answered

1. Dishonesty with God

"There is another matter too often neglected by those who seek the Lord in **prayer**. Have you been honest with God? By the prophet Malachi the Lord declares, *Even from the days of your fathers ye are gone away from Mine ordinances, and have not kept them. Return unto Me, and I will return unto you, saith the LORD of hosts. But ye said, Wherein shall we return? Will a man rob God? Yet ye have robbed Me. But ye say, Wherein have we robbed Thee? In tithes and offerings.*—Malachi 3:7-8 KJV.

"As the Giver of every blessing, God claims a certain portion of all we possess. This is His provision to sustain the preaching of the gospel. And by making this return to God, we are to show our appreciation of His gifts. But if we withhold from Him that which is His own, how can we claim His blessing? If we are unfaithful stewards of earthly things, how can we expect Him to entrust us with the things of heaven? It may be that here is the secret of answered prayer." [62]

> **Reflection Thoughts**—Are there areas in your life that you have *unwillingly or unknowingly* been **dishonest** with God? Pray and ask God to show you those areas, then humbly **ASK** forgiveness for what He reveals to you. **THANK** Him for the revelation and **BELIEVE** that you are forgiven. Record your thoughts in your personal journal or on your **Reflections** page.

2. Lack of Persistence in Prayers

"...We must show a firm, undeviating trust in God. Often He delays to answer us in order to try our faith or test the genuineness of our desire. Having asked according to His Word, we should believe His promise and press our petitions with a determination that will not be denied.

God does not say, Ask once, and you shall receive. He bids us ask. Unwearyingly persist in prayer. The persistent asking brings the petitioner into a more earnest attitude, and gives him an increased desire to receive the things for which he asks. "If thou wouldest believe, thou shouldest see the glory of God." But many have not a living faith. This is why they do not see more of the power of God. Their weakness is the result of their unbelief." [63]

> **Reflection Thoughts**—Are there times when you have prayed and when the answer did not come, you gave up? What can you do to renew your faith? His Word bids us ASK persistently. Record your thoughts in your personal journal or your Reflections page.

Hindrances to Answered Prayer

Introduction

God is so anxious for us to understand the concept of claiming His **promises** and working in partnership with Him, that He tells us the **conditions**—in the positive and then reiterates them in the negative …including, within the context of scripture, statements like, *I will not hear you* or *I will turn a deaf ear* or *I will turn My back.* God's blessings and curses are alike conditional.

If we are unwilling to obey God, why should we expect Him to answer our petitions? Our Father wants to shower us with blessings. First He wants no breach in our relationship with Him, because He loves us and we are the *apple of His eye.*—Psalm 17:8

The following is a list of **Hindrances to Answered Prayer**. If you find yourself convicted of anything on the list, go before God in repentance. These **promises** are not to cause you to lose hope, but to direct you and encourage you as to what changes you may need to make in your life in order to assure that the Lord will listen. God wants us in right relationship with Him. He is anxious to forgive and help you start afresh. Having everything right between you and Him is what Jesus' victory on the cross was to accomplish. "When we come to Him confessing our unworthiness and sin, He has pledged Himself to give heed to our cry. The honor of His throne is staked for the fulfillment of His word to us."[64]

Hindrances

1. **Reject God vs. Feel Our Need of God**

   Read **1 Samuel 8:18** and paraphrase it here: _____

   _____

   Read **Proverbs 1:22-33** and paraphrase verse **28** here: _____

   _____

2. **Unfaithfulness vs. Ask in Jesus' Name**

Read **Psalm 78:57-58** and paraphrase them here: _____

_____

3. **Instability vs. Perseverance**   4. **Instability vs. Diligence**

Read **James 1:6-8** and paraphrase them here: _____

_____

"The more earnestly and steadfastly we ask, the closer will be our spiritual union with Christ. We shall receive increased blessings because we have increased faith.

"Our part is to pray and believe. Watch unto prayer. Watch, and cooperate with the prayer-hearing God."

Read **1 Corinthians 3:9** and paraphrase it here: _____

_____

"Speak and act in harmony with your prayers. It will ... prove your faith to be genuine, or show that your prayers are only a form ... Never allow yourself to talk in a hopeless, discouraged way. If you do you will lose much ... Talk and act as if your faith was invincible. The Lord is rich in resources; He owns the world. Look heavenward in faith. Look to Him who has light and power and efficiency."[65]

5. **Seek Other Gods vs. Seek First Kingdom of God**

Read **Jeremiah 11:13-14** and paraphrase them here: _____

_____

6. **Rebellious vs. Responsive Heart**

   Read **Deuteronomy 1:43-45** and paraphrase them here: _____

   _____

   Read **Zechariah 7:13** and paraphrase it here: _____

   _____

7. **Arrogance vs. Humility/Repentance**

   Read **Job 35:12-13** and paraphrase it here: _____

   _____

   _____

8. **Disobedience vs. Obedience**

   Read **Jeremiah 7:13-16** and paraphrase them here: _____

   _____

   Read **Proverbs 28:9** and paraphrase it here: _____

   _____

   Read 1 **Samuel 28:6** and paraphrase it here: _____

   _____

"If we are disobedient, we bring to the Lord a note to be cashed when we have not fulfilled the conditions that would make it payable to us. We present to God His promises, and ask Him to fulfill them, when by so doing He would dishonor His own name."[66]

9. **Lack of Faith vs. Faith**

   Read **James 1:6** and paraphrase it here: _____

   _____

   _____

   "But we must show a firm, undeviating trust in God. Often He delays to answer us in order to try our faith or test the genuineness of our desire. Having asked according to His word, we should believe His promise and press our petitions with a determination that will not be denied."[67]

10. **Impatient vs. Patient**

    Read **Isaiah 59:1-2** and paraphrase them here: _____

    _____

    _____

    When we are impatient, not willing to wait upon God, and we take things into our own hands, we sin. Sin separates.

11. **Hate vs. Love**

    Read **Ezekiel 8:17-18** and paraphrase them here: _____

    _____

    _____

    Read **Isaiah 1:15** and paraphrase it here:_____

    _____

12. Unforgiving Heart vs. Forgiveness

Read **Matthew 6:14-15** and paraphrase them here: _____

_____

_____

13. Selfish Motives/Neglect of Mercy vs. Concern for Others

Read **James 4:3** and paraphrase it here: _____

_____

Read **Proverbs 21:13** and paraphrase it here: _____

_____

"Our prayers are not to be a selfish asking, merely for our own benefit. We are to ask that we may give. The principle of Christ's life must be the principle of our lives ... The same devotion, the same self-sacrifice, the same subjection to the claims of the word of God, that were manifest in Christ, must be seen in His servants. Our mission to the world is not to serve or please ourselves; we are to glorify God by cooperating with Him to save sinners. We are to ask blessings from God that we may communicate to others. The capacity for receiving is preserved only by imparting. We cannot continue to receive heavenly treasure without communicating to those around us."[68]

14. Cherished Sin vs. Pure Heart

Read **Psalm 66:18** and paraphrase it here: _____

_____

Read Isaiah 59:2 and paraphrase it here: _____

_____

Read Micah 3:4 and paraphrase it here: _____

_____

Hindrance for Married Couples/Dishonoring to Spouse

Read **1 Peter 3:7** and paraphrase it here: _____

_____

May we continue to grow in Jesus as we incorporate God's promises into our devotional life. By claiming the conditions as promises and calling upon His enabling to do our part, we will experience the fulfillment/gift according to God's timing and destiny for our life.

If Jesus needed to pray in order to deal with the things that He faced, how much more do we? Jesus example makes it abundantly clear how central prayer needs to be in our walk with the Lord. If communication is crucial to maintaining relationships with other people, how much more so in a relationship with God? The question is: How consistent is your prayer life?

Mid Study Review

You have now reached the halfway point of this study. Everything you have learned so far should now be a permanent and integral part of your prayer life.

I encourage you to take the time to complete this mid-book review. If you find yourself unsure of the answers, I would recommend reviewing those points. The answers for this review can be found in Appendix A.

1. We have been studying the Prayer of _____, also known

   as the Prayer of _____ or _____.

2. The three Vocal Conditions to claiming *Bible* Promises are
   Extra points if you can remember the text for each!

   _____   _____   _____

3. Name the 15 General Conditions in claiming *Bible* Promises.

   _____   _____   _____

   _____   _____   _____

   _____   _____   _____

   _____   _____   _____

   _____   _____   _____

4. There are approximately (circle one) Promises or clusters of Promises in the *Bible*.

   a. 1000   b. 3000   c. 5000   d. 7000

5. Name two objectives of this class: _____

   _____

   _____

6. Name two ways to guard against presumption when claiming God's Promises.

   _____

   _____

Assignment

1. Pray the prayers on the **Daily Prayer Sheet**

   ### For Forgiveness

   Dear Heavenly Father,

   I **ask** that You will forgive me for _____;

   I **believe** that You have forgiven me because You have promised in 1 John 1:9;

   I **thank** You that You have forgiven me.

   In Jesus' name, Amen.

   ### For Intercession and Soul Winning

   Dear Heavenly Father,

   I **ask** that You will give me life to give _____;

   I **believe** that You are giving me life to give him/her because You have promised in 1 John 5:16;

   I **thank** You that You have given me life to give him/her.

   In Jesus' name, Amen.

   ### For the Holy Spirit

   Dear Heavenly Father,

   I **ask** that You will give me the Holy Spirit;

   I **believe** that You are giving me the Holy Spirit because You have promised in Luke 11:13;

   I **thank** You that You have given me the Holy Spirit.

   In Jesus' name, Amen.

2. *Bible* Promises for your personal needs

   Find five *Bible* **promises** for your personal needs using the list in Appendix A or a Concordance.

   It is important to pray the promises set out in God's Word. Use the Record of Experience to record the Scriptures that the Holy Spirit reveals to you and how they apply to the personal problems that you may be having at this time.

3. What do the following texts teach us about Jesus and prayer? What is the context of each verse?

Matthew 14:23

_____

Matthew 26:34-44

_____

Luke 3:21-22

_____

Luke 6:12-13

_____

Luke 9:28-29

_____

Luke 22:31-32

_____

Hebrews 5:7

_____

4. Read _Consecration_ on the following pages

5. Journal on the **Reflections** page

   Using your own personal journal or the **Reflections** page, record how the reading of _Consecration_ changed you and your approach to life and/or some of the important points that spoke to you from your reading.

Consecration

God's promise is *You will seek me, and you will find me because you will seek me with all your heart.*—Jeremiah 29:13 GNB.

We must give all of our heart to God, or we cannot be changed to be like Him. Our sinful hearts are unlike God, and naturally turn from Him. The *Bible* describes the way we are: *spiritually dead; your heart and mind are sick; not a healthy spot on your body.*—Ephesians 2:1; Isaiah 1:5-6. Sinners are held fast by Satan. They are in *the trap of the Devil, who had caught them and made them obey his will.*—2 Timothy 2:26 GNB.

God wants to heal us. He wants to set us free. To do this He must change us entirely so that we have new desires and habits. But He cannot do this until we give ourselves completely to Him.

The battle against self is the greatest battle ever fought. It is hard for us to give ourselves to God and let Him control our minds. But we must let God rule or He cannot make us new and holy.

Satan wants us to believe that we will be slaves in God's kingdom, blindly submitting to unreasonable demands. He says that God asks us to obey Him without giving reasons for His commands. But this is not true. We serve God with our reason as well as our conscience. God says to the people He has made, "Come now, and let us reason together." Isaiah 1:18, KJV. God does not force us to obey. He cannot accept our worship unless we give it freely and with the mind.

Being forced to obey God would prevent us from developing our minds and characters. We would be like machines, and this is not what our Creator wants. He wants us, the crowning work of Creation, to make the best possible use of our minds and bodies. He teaches us about the great blessings He wants to bring us through His grace.

God invites us to give ourselves to Him so that He may guide us and carry out His plans for us. He gives us the right to choose what we shall do. We may choose to be set free from sin and share in the wonderful liberty that He gives His children.

When we give ourselves to God, we give up all that would separate us from Him. The Savior said, *None of you can be my disciple unless you give up everything you have.*—Luke 14:33 GNB. We must give up everything that takes our hearts away from God.

Many people worship riches. The desire for wealth and the love of money bind them to Satan. Others desire honor more than anything else. They want people to look up to them and praise them. Still others wish for an easy, selfish life with freedom from care. But we must turn away from all these. We cannot belong half to God and half to the world. We are God's children only when we are entirely His.

Some people say that they serve God, but they try to obey His laws without His help. By their own works they try to develop a good character and receive salvation. Their hearts are not moved by the love of Christ. They try to do good works because they think God requires this in order for them to reach heaven. Such religion is worth nothing.

When Christ lives in us, we will be filled with His love. The joy of His friendship will make us want to be near Him. We shall think about Him so much that we will forget our selfish desires. Love for Him will guide every action. If we feel the love of God, we will not ask how little we can do to obey Him. We will try to do all that our Redeemer wants. People who say they are Christians and do not feel deep love for Christ are using words without meaning. To follow Christ is hard work for them.

Should we feel it is too much to give all to Christ? We must ask ourselves the question, "What has Christ given for me?" The Son of God gave all—life and love and suffering—to save us. Can we, who are not worth this great love, keep back our hearts from Him?

Every moment of our lives we have received the blessings of His grace. Because of this we can never really know from how much trouble we have been saved. Can we look at the One who died for our sins and turn from such love? Our Lord of glory humbled Himself. Shall we complain because we must fight against selfishness and be humble?

Many proud hearts are asking, "Why do I need to humble myself and be sorry for my sins before I am sure that God will accept me?" I point you to Christ. He was sinless. He was the Prince of heaven, and yet He took our place and carried all our sins. *He willingly gave his life and shared the fate of evil men. He took the place of many sinners and prayed that they might be forgiven.*—Isaiah 53:12 GNT.

What do we give when we give Him everything? We give Jesus a sinful heart for Him to make pure and clean. We ask Him to save us by His infinite love. And yet people think it is hard to give up all! I am ashamed to hear these words spoken; I am ashamed to write them.

God does not ask us to give up anything that is good for us to keep. He is thinking of what is best for us. I wish that all who have not chosen Christ could realize this. Christ has something far better for them than they could ask for themselves. People are not being fair to themselves when they go against what God wants.

We can find no real joy in walking in the path He tells us not to take. He knows what is good for us, and He has the best plan for each person. The path of disobeying God is the path of unhappiness and death.

Do not think that God likes to see His children suffer. All heaven is interested in our happiness. Our heavenly Father does not keep us from doing anything that will bring us true joy. He asks us to turn away from wrong habits and other things that will bring us suffering. He knows they will keep us from happiness and heaven.

The world's Redeemer accepts people as they are, with all their weaknesses and many faults. But He will wash away their sins and redeem them through His blood. He will satisfy the desires of all who are willing to bear His load and share His work. He wants to give peace and rest to all who come to Him. He asks them to do only those things that will lead to great happiness. Those who do not obey cannot know this pleasure. True joy is to have Christ, the hope of glory, in the life.

Many people are asking, "*How* can I give myself to God?" They want to give themselves to Him, but their moral strength is weak. They doubt God and are controlled by sinful habits. Their promises are easily broken, like ropes of sand. They cannot control their thoughts or their desires. Because they cannot keep their promises, they lose confidence in themselves and wonder if they are sincere. They feel that God cannot accept them. But they must not lose hope.

We all need to understand the value of willpower. The power of choice is the ruling power in life. Everything depends on the right use of this power. God has given the power of choice to each person, and it is theirs to use. We cannot change our hearts. We cannot by ourselves give our love to God. But we can *choose* to serve Him. We can give Him the powers of our mind. Then He will help us choose the right way. Our whole being will be guided by the Spirit of Christ. We will love God, and our thoughts will be like His.

It is right that we should desire to be good and to be holy. But we must not stop there. These desires will not help us. Many people will be lost while hoping and desiring to be Christians. They do not come to the place where they yield the powers of the mind to God. They do not *choose* to be Christians.

An entire change may be made in our lives through the right use of the power of choice. When we put ourselves on God's side, He gives us His great power to hold us. By giving ourselves to God each day we will be able to live a new life, the life of faith.[69]

Record of Experiences

Record of Experiences

This record of experiences will help you keep a list of the problems you had, the promises you claimed and the date your prayers were answered. It will help to increase your faith in the future when you can look back and see how God so miraculously intervened.

Date Asked	Problem	Promise Text	Date Answered	How Answered

Speak Lord, Your servant is listening—1 Samuel 3:9-10 NIV

Weekly Reflections

_____

_____

_____

_____

_____

_____

_____

_____

_____

_____

_____

_____

"When we do not know God's will, this as never before is the time to reach toward Heaven and give him our hand. By doing so, we are letting go and letting God."

—*Praying in the "YES" of God*, p 184

LESSON SIX—PRAYER OF COMMITMENT

... nevertheless not My will, but Yours, be done.
—Luke 22:42

(Please refer to pages 179-186 in **Living Volume One: Praying in the "YES" of God** while studying this chapter.)

In Lesson One we learned that there are two types of prayers of faith: (1) The **Prayer of Reception** (**Faith, Petition**), and (2) The **Prayer of Commitment**. We have spent our time up to now studying the **Prayer of Reception** and the science of appropriating God's **promises** to our lives. In this lesson we will study more about praying the **Prayer of Commitment**.

The Prayer of Commitment

WHAT THE PRAYER OF COMMITMENT IS:

1. This is a **prayer** of **committal** to God's will—*Not my will but Thine be done.*

Growing in the "YES" of God

2. **Prayed** when we are not sure of God's will.

   Read **1 John 5:14** and paraphrase it here: _____

   _____

WHEN TO PRAY THE PRAYER OF COMMITMENT:

1. When we are not sure of God's will.

   We must **commit** our will to God's will when we have no **promise** for a particular problem beyond the one in Matthew 7:7 *Ask, and it will be given you; seek, and you will find, knock, and it will be opened to you.*

   Note: When we **pray** the **Prayer of Reception** we already know God's will because it is specifically stated in the **promise**. There are, however, times when we have specific requests but no **promises** to reveal God's will. For example: choosing a certain house to live in, choosing life work, choosing a life companion, etc. We must **pray** the **Prayer of Commitment** then.

2. When we are **praying** for the healing of the sick.

   "It is not always safe to ask for unconditional healing. Let your **prayer** include this thought: 'Lord, thou knowest every secret of the soul. Thou art acquainted with these persons; for Jesus, their Advocate, gave His life for them. He loves them better than we possibly can. If, therefore, it is for Thy glory and the good of these afflicted ones to raise them up to health, we ask Thee, in the name of Jesus, that health may be given them at this time. In a petition of this kind, no lack of faith is manifested."[70]

   Read **Lamentation 3:33** and paraphrase it here: _____

   _____

   Read **Psalm 103:13** and paraphrase it here: _____

   _____

"He knows our heart, for He reads every secret of the soul. He knows whether or not those for whom petitions are offered would be able to endure the trial and test that would come to them if they lived. He knows the end from the beginning. Many will be laid away to sleep before the fiery ordeal of the time of trouble shall come upon our world. This is another reason why we should say after our earnest petition: *Nevertheless, not my will, but Thine be done.*—Luke 22:42 KJV. Such a petition will never be registered in heaven as a faithless **prayer**."[71]

Read **Isaiah 57:1-2** and paraphrase it here: _____

_____

_____

"In **praying** for the sick, we are to **pray** that, if it is God's will, they may be raised up to health; but if not that He will give them His grace to comfort, His presence to sustain them in their suffering ... All that we are required to do is to **ask** God to raise the sick up if in accordance with His will, **believing** that He hears the reasons which we present and the fervent **prayers** offered. If the Lord sees it will best honor Him, He will answer our **prayers**. But to urge recovery without submission to His will, is not right. We are to keep on **asking**, even if we do not realize the immediate response to our **prayers**."[72]

BASIC PRINCIPLES REGARDING SICKNESS AND HEALTH

1. **We reap what we sow—this is the law of cause and effect.**

Read **Galatians 6:7-8** and paraphrase them here: _____

_____

_____

"By the laws of God in nature, effect follows cause with unvarying certainty." [73]

Growing in the "YES" of God

2. **God will not protect us from our abuses of His laws.**

   Read **Galatians 6:7** and paraphrase it here: _____

   _____

   "Every seed sown produces a harvest of its kind. So it is in human life... Every characteristic of selfishness, self-love, self-esteem, every act of self-indulgence, will bring forth a like harvest. God destroys no man. Everyone who is destroyed will have destroyed himself... As the seed sown produces a harvest, and this in turn is sown, the harvest is multiplied." [74]

   Read **1 Corinthians 6:19** and paraphrase it here: _____

   _____

3. **Most sickness is the result of our disobeying the physical, mental, or moral laws, whether ignorantly or intentionally**.

   "To many of the afflicted ones who received healing, Christ said, *"Go and sin no more, lest a worse thing come unto thee.*—John 5:14. Thus He taught that disease is the result of violating God's laws, both natural and spiritual. The great misery in the world would not exist did men but live in harmony with the Creator's plan." [75]

   "...all sickness is a result of transgression. Many are suffering in consequence of the transgression of their parents. They cannot be censured for their parents' sin; but it is nevertheless their duty to ascertain wherein their parents violated the laws of their being which has entailed upon their offspring so miserable an inheritance—and wherein their parents' habits were wrong, they should change their course, and place themselves by correct habits in a better relation to health." [76]

   a. Ninety percent of all diseases originate in the mind because of mental depression and negative thinking.

      "Satan is the originator of disease; and the physician is warring against his work and power. Sickness of the mind prevails everywhere. Nine tenths of the diseases from which men suffer have their foundation here."[77]

b. "The condition of the mind affects the health to a far greater degree than many realize. Many of the diseases from which men suffer are the result of mental depression. Grief, anxiety, discontent, remorse, guilt, distrust, all tend to break down the life forces and to invite decay and death."[78]

c. The mind must be kept looking out and up for positive thinking to take place.

Read **Proverbs 17:22** and paraphrase it here: _____

_____

Read **Nehemiah 8:10** and paraphrase it here: _____

_____

We are to take our eyes off ourselves and look to Jesus. Praise dispels the enemy. God inhabits the praises of His people. And God promises joy and peace as we keep our mind on Him. Don't worry about anything, pray about everything; tell God your needs and thank Him for His answers. Think about things that are pure and lovely, and dwell on the fine, good things in others. Think about all you can praise God for, and be glad about.

"If you do not feel lighthearted and joyous, do not talk out your feelings...Instead of thinking of your discouragements, think of the power you can claim in Christ's name ...Let your thoughts be directed to the evidences of the great love of God for you."[79]

"It is not wise to look to ourselves and study our emotions. If we do this, the enemy will present difficulties and temptations that weaken faith and destroy our courage... We are to look away from ourselves to Jesus...It is a positive duty to resist melancholy, discontented thoughts and feelings—as much a duty as it is to pray. ... When someone asks how you are feeling, do not try to think of something mournful to tell in order to gain sympathy. Do not talk of your lack of faith and your sorrows and sufferings."[80]

Growing in the "YES" of God

OBEDIENCE TO THE LAWS OF NATURE AND PHYSIOLOGY IS THE KEY TO GOOD PHYSICAL AND MENTAL HEALTH.

Read **Deuteronomy 7:12-15** and paraphrase them here: _____

_____

_____

"Had they (the Israelites) been willing to deny appetite, in obedience to His wise restrictions, feebleness and disease would have been unknown among them. Their descendants would have possessed both physical and mental strength. They would have had clear perceptions of truth and duty, keen discriminations, and sound judgment."[81]

Read **Proverbs 3:1-8** and paraphrase them here: _____

_____

_____

Don't worry about anything; instead, pray about everything; tell God your needs and don't forget to thank Him for His answers. If you do this you will experience God's peace which is far more wonderful than the human mind can understand. His peace will keep your thoughts and your heart quiet and at rest as you trust in Christ Jesus ... Fix your thoughts on what is true and good and right. Think about things that are pure and lovely and dwell on the fine, good things in others. Think about all you can praise God for, and be glad about.—Philippians 4:6-8 TLB.

Reflections Thoughts—Ask God to search your heart and reveal any changes you need to make in your personal health care and life style. Record your thoughts in your personal journal or your **Reflections** page.

---

1. "Many have inquired of me, 'What course shall I take to best preserve my health?' My answer is **make sure you are not neglecting these needs of your body**:(Source: Weimar Institute Newstart Program)

   N   Nutrition

   E   Exercise

   W   Water

   S   Sunshine

   T   Temperance

   A   Fresh Air

   R   Rest

   T   Trust in God

   "Result: you will not be sick."[82]

   These elements require harmonious integration in the life. If we over-emphasize any of them to the neglect of the others we will not have a balanced program of healthful living.[83]

   "A practical knowledge of the science of human life is necessary in order to glorify God in our bodies."[84]

2. **Learn the laws of nature and physiology.**

   "It is the duty of every person, for his own sake, and for the sake of humanity, to inform himself in regard to the laws of life, and conscientiously to obey them. All need to become acquainted with that most wonderful of all organisms, the human body. They should understand the functions of the various organs and the dependence of one upon another for the healthy action of all. They should study the influence of the mind upon the body, and of the body upon the mind, and the laws by which they are governed."[85]

"So closely is health related to our happiness, that we cannot have the latter without the former. A practical knowledge of the science of human life is necessary in order to glorify God in our bodies. It is therefore of the highest importance that among the studies selected for childhood, physiology should occupy the first place. How few know anything about the structure and functions of their own bodies and of nature's laws!"[86]

3. **Those requesting prayer for divine healing should be taught the laws of health and healing.**

"To those who desire prayer for their restoration of health, it should be made plain that the violation of God's law either natural or spiritual, is sin, and that in order for them to receive His blessing, sin must be confessed and forsaken ... It is labor lost to teach people to look to God as a healer of their infirmities, unless they are taught also to lay aside unhealthful practices. In order to receive His blessing, in answer to prayer, they must cease to do evil and learn to do well. Their surroundings must be sanitary, their habits of life correct. They must live in harmony with the laws of God, both natural and spiritual."[87]

4. **Healing Promises are for every emergency and every trial.**

"Seek the Lord for wisdom in every emergency. In every trial plead with Jesus to show you a way out of your troubles, then your eyes will be opened to behold the remedy and to apply to your case the healing promises that have been recorded in His word. In this way the enemy will find no place to lead you into mourning and unbelief, but instead you will have faith and courage in the Lord."[88]

Assignment

1. Pray the prayers on the **Daily Prayer Sheet**

   For Forgiveness

   > Dear Heavenly Father,
   >
   > I **ask** that You will forgive me for._____;
   >
   > I **believe** that You have forgiven me because You have promised in 1 John 1:9;
   >
   > I **thank** You that You have forgiven me.
   >
   > In Jesus' name, Amen.

   For Intercession and Soul Winning

   > Dear Heavenly Father,
   >
   > I **ask** that You will give me life to give _____;
   >
   > I **believe** that You are giving me life to give him/her because You have promised in 1 John 5:16;
   >
   > I **thank** You that You have given me life to give him/her.
   >
   > In Jesus' name, Amen.

   For the Holy Spirit

   > Dear Heavenly Father,
   >
   > I **ask** that You will give me the Holy Spirit;
   >
   > I **believe** that You are giving me the Holy Spirit because You have promised in Luke 11:13;
   >
   > I **thank** You that You have given me the Holy Spirit.
   >
   > In Jesus' name, Amen.

2. Find, record, and claim daily five *Bible* Promises that deal with **healing** or **health** problems that you could use for yourself or share with a friend in trouble. Some healing promises may be found in the list in Appendix A. You will find a much more detailed resource for *Bible* Promises for **Health** and **Healing** in Derry's book *Heaven Touches Earth: Handbook for Supporting Sick, Terminally Ill and Dying* and *Heaven Touches Earth: Healing and Deliverance Scriptures*. Both books are available on Derry's website: FreedomInSurrender.net

3. Read *Prayer for the Sick* on the following pages and journal your thoughts on how this reading changed you and your approach to life.

4. In preparation for Chapter 7, read pages 187-193 in *Living Volume One: Praying in the "YES" of God*.

Prayer for the Sick

The Scripture says that *men always ought to pray and not lose heart.*—Luke 18:1. If ever there is a time when people feel their need of prayer, it is when strength fails and life itself seems slipping from their grasp. Often those who are in health forget the wonderful mercies extended to them day by day, year after year, and they render no tribute of praise to God for His benefits. But when sickness comes, God is remembered. When human strength fails, people feel their need of divine help. And never does our merciful God turn from the soul that in sincerity seeks Him for help. He is our refuge in sickness as in health.

As a father pities his children, So the Lord pities those who fear Him. For He knows our frame; He remembers that we are dust.—Psalm 103:13-14.

Because of their transgression, And because of their iniquities, [people] were afflicted. Their soul abhorred all manner of food, And they drew near to the gates of death. Then they cried out to the Lord in their trouble, And He saved them out of their distresses. He sent His word and healed them, And delivered them from their destructions.—Psalm 107:17-20.

God is just as willing to restore the sick to health now as when the Holy Spirit spoke these words through the psalmist. And Christ is the same compassionate Physician now that He was during His earthly ministry. In Him there is healing balm for every disease, restoring power for every infirmity. His disciples in this time are to pray for the sick as verily as the disciples of old prayed. And recoveries will follow, for "the prayer of faith will save the sick." We have the Holy Spirit's power, the calm assurance of faith, that can claim God's promises.

The Lord's promise, *They will lay hands on the sick, and they will recover.*—Mark 16:18, is just as trustworthy now as in the days of the apostles. It presents the privilege of God's children, and our faith should lay hold of all that it embraces. Christ's servants are the channel of His working, and through them He desires to exercise His healing power. It is our work to present the sick and suffering to God in the arms of our faith. We should teach them to believe in the Great Healer.

The Savior would have us encourage the sick, the hopeless, the afflicted, to take hold upon His strength. Through faith and prayer the sickroom may be transformed into a Bethel. In word and deed, physicians and nurses may say, so plainly that it cannot be misunderstood, "God is in this place" to save, and not to destroy. Christ desires to manifest His presence in the sickroom, filling the hearts of physicians and nurses with the sweetness of His love. If the life of those who attend the sick is such that Christ can go with them to the bedside of the patient, there will come to the sick the conviction that the compassionate Savior is present, and this conviction will itself do much for the healing of both soul and body.

God hears prayer. Christ has said, *If you ask anything in My name, I will do it.* Again He says, *If anyone serves Me, him My Father will honor.*—John 14:14; 12:26. If we live according to His Word, every precious promise He has given will be fulfilled to us. We are undeserving of His mercy, but as we give ourselves to Him, He receives us. He will work for and through those who follow Him.

But only as we live in obedience to His Word can we claim the fulfillment of His promises. The psalmist says, *If I regard iniquity in my heart, the Lord will not hear.*—Psalm 66:18. If we render to Him only a partial, halfhearted obedience, His promises will not be fulfilled to us.

In the Word of God we have instruction relative to special prayer for the recovery of the sick. The offering of such prayer is a most solemn act and should not be entered upon without careful consideration. In many cases of prayer for healing of the sick, that which is called faith is nothing less than presumption.

Abandon Unhealthful Practices

Many persons bring disease upon themselves by self-indulgence. They have not lived in accordance with natural law or the principles of strict purity. Others have disregarded the laws of health in their habits of eating and drinking, dressing, or working. Often some form of vice is the cause of feebleness of mind or body. If these persons were to gain the blessing of health, many of them would continue to pursue the same course of heedless transgression of God's natural and spiritual laws. They would reason that if God heals them in answer to prayer, they are at liberty to continue their unhealthful practices and to indulge perverted appetite. If God were to work a miracle in restoring these persons to health, He would be encouraging sin.

It is labor lost to teach people to look to God as a healer of their infirmities unless they are taught also to lay aside unhealthful practices. In order to receive His blessing in answer to prayer, they must cease to do evil and learn to do well. Their surroundings must be sanitary, their habits of life correct. They must live in harmony with the law of God, both natural and spiritual.

Confession of Sin

To those who desire prayer for restoration to health, it should be made plain that the violation of God's law, either natural or spiritual, is sin, and that in order for them to receive His blessing, sin must be confessed and forsaken.

The Scripture bids us, *Confess your trespasses to one another, and pray for one another, that you may be healed.*—James 5:16. To the one asking for prayer, let thoughts like these be presented: "We cannot read the heart or know the secrets of your life. These are known only to yourself and to God. If you repent of your sins, it is your duty to confess them." Sin of a private character is to be confessed to Christ, the only mediator between God and man. For *if anyone sins, we have an Advocate with the Father, Jesus Christ the righteous.*—1 John 2:1. Every sin is an offense against God and is to be confessed to Him through Christ.

Every open sin should be as openly confessed. Wrong done to a fellow being should be made right with the one who has been offended. If any who are seeking health have been guilty of evil speaking, if they have sowed discord in the home, the neighborhood, or the church and have stirred up alienation and dissension, if by any wrong practice they have led others into sin, these things should be confessed before God and before those who have been offended. *If we confess our sins, He is faithful and just to forgive us our sins and to cleanse us from all unrighteousness.*—1 John 1:9.

When wrongs have been righted, we may present the needs of the sick to the Lord in calm faith, as His Spirit may indicate. He knows each person by name and cares for each as if there were not another upon the earth for whom He gave His beloved Son. Because God's love is so great and so unfailing, the sick should be encouraged to trust in Him and be cheerful. To be anxious about themselves tends to cause weakness and disease. If they will rise above depression and gloom, their prospect of recovery will be better, for *the eye of the Lord is on those ... who hope in His mercy.*— Psalm 33:18.

God Knows Best

In prayer for the sick it should be remembered that *we do not know what we should pray for as we ought.*—Romans 8:26. We do not know whether the blessing we desire will be best. Therefore our prayers should include this thought: "Lord, you know every secret of the soul. You are acquainted with these persons. Jesus, their Advocate, gave His life for them. His love for them is greater than ours can possibly be. If, therefore, it is for Your glory and the good of the afflicted ones, we ask, in the name of Jesus, that they may be restored to health. If it is not Your will that they may be restored, we ask that Your grace may comfort and Your presence sustain them in their sufferings."

God knows the end from the beginning. He is acquainted with the hearts of all human beings. He reads every secret of the soul. He knows whether those for whom prayer is offered would be able to endure the trials that would come upon them should they live. He knows whether their lives would be a blessing or a curse to themselves and to the world. This is one reason why, while presenting our petitions with earnestness, we should say, *Nevertheless not my will, but Yours, be done.*—Luke 22:42. Jesus added these words of submission to the wisdom and will of God when in the Garden of Gethsemane He pleaded, *O My Father, if it is possible, let this cup pass from Me.*—Matthew 26:39. And if they were appropriate for Him, the Son of God, how much more appropriate are they on the lips of finite, erring mortals!

The consistent course is to commit our desires to our all-wise heavenly Father, and then, in perfect confidence, trust all to Him. We know that God hears us if we ask according to His will. But to press our petitions without a submissive spirit is not right. Our prayers must take the form, not of command, but of intercession.

There are cases where God works decidedly by His divine power in the restoration of health. But not all the sick are healed. Many are laid away to sleep in Jesus. John on the Isle of Patmos was bidden to write: "*Blessed are the dead who die in the Lord from now on. Yes,* says the Spirit, *that they may rest from their labors, and their works follow them.*"—Revelation 14:13. From this we see that if persons are not raised to health, they should not on this account be judged as lacking in faith.

We all desire immediate and direct answers to our prayers and are tempted to become discouraged when the answer is delayed or comes in an unlooked-for form. But God is too wise and too good to answer our prayers always at just the time and in just the way we desire. He will do more and better for us than to accomplish all our wishes. And because we can trust His wisdom and love, we should not ask Him to concede to our will but should seek to enter into and accomplish His purpose. Our desires and interests should be lost in His will. These experiences that test faith are for our benefit. They reveal whether our faith is true and sincere, resting on the Word of God alone, or whether, depending on circumstances, it is uncertain and changeable. Faith is strengthened by exercise. We must let patience have its perfect work, remembering that there are precious promises in the Scriptures for those who wait upon the Lord.

Not all understand these principles. Many who seek the Lord's healing mercy think that they must have a direct and immediate answer to their prayers or their faith is defective. For this reason, those who are weakened by disease need to be counseled wisely, that they may act with discretion. They should not disregard their duty to the friends who may survive them, or neglect to employ nature's agencies for the restoration of health.

Often there is danger of error here. Believing that they will be healed in answer to prayer, some fear to do anything that might seem to indicate a lack of faith. But they should not neglect to set their affairs in order as they would desire to do if they expected to be removed by death. Nor should they fear to utter words of encouragement or counsel that at the parting hour they wish to speak to their loved ones.

Employ Remedial Agencies

Those who seek healing by prayer should not neglect to make use of the remedial agencies within their reach. It is not a denial of faith to use such remedies as God has provided to alleviate pain and to aid nature in her work of restoration. It is no denial of faith to cooperate with God and to place themselves in the condition most favorable to recovery. God has put it in our power to obtain a knowledge of the laws of life. This knowledge has been placed within our reach for use. We should employ every facility for the restoration of health, taking every advantage possible, working in harmony with natural laws. When we have prayed for the recovery of the sick, we can work with all the more energy, thanking God that we have the privilege of cooperating with Him, and asking His blessing on the means that He Himself has provided.

Growing in the "YES" of God

We have the sanction of the Word of God for the use of remedial agencies. Hezekiah, king of Israel, was sick, and a prophet of God brought him the message that he would die. He cried to the Lord, and the Lord heard His servant and sent him a message that fifteen years would be added to his life. One word from God would have healed Hezekiah instantly, but special directions were given, *Let them take a lump of figs, and apply it as a poultice on the boil, and he shall recover.*—Isaiah 38:21.

On one occasion Christ used clay to anoint the eyes of a blind man and told him, *'Go, wash in the pool of Siloam'. ... So he went and washed, and came back seeing.*—John 9:7. The cure could be wrought only by the power of the Great Healer, yet Christ made use of the simple agencies of nature. He did not give approval for drug medication, but He sanctioned the use of simple and natural remedies.

When we have prayed for the recovery of the sick, whatever the outcome, let us not lose faith in God. If we are called upon to meet bereavement, let us accept the bitter cup, remembering that a Father's hand holds it to our lips. But if health is restored, it should not be forgotten that the recipient of healing mercy is placed under renewed obligation to the Creator.

When the ten lepers were cleansed, only one returned to find Jesus and give Him glory. Let none of us be like the unthinking nine, whose hearts were untouched by the mercy of God. *Every good gift and every perfect gift is from above, and comes down from the Father of lights, with whom there is no variation or shadow of turning.*—James 1:17.[89]

112

Record of Experiences

Record of Experiences

This record of experiences will help you keep a list of the problems you had, the promises you claimed and the date your prayers were answered. It will help to increase your faith in the future when you can look back and see how God so miraculously intervened.

Date Asked	Problem	Promise Text	Date Answered	How Answered

Growing in the "YES" of God

Speak Lord, Your servant is listening—1 Samuel 3:9-10 NIV

Weekly Reflections

_____

_____

_____

_____

_____

_____

_____

_____

_____

_____

_____

"The imperative questions: Do you want to possess the Holy Spirit, or do you want the Holy Spirit to possess you? Are you willing to respond in heartfelt obedience?"

—*Praying in the "YES" of God*, p. 170

LESSON SEVEN—THE HOLY SPIRIT

If you then, being evil, know how to give good gifts to your children, how much more will your Heavenly Father give the Holy Spirit to those who ask Him!

—Luke 11:13

(Please refer to pages 61-67 in **Living Volume One: Praying in the "YES" of God** *while you are studying this chapter.)*

Introduction

What we have studied so far:

1. The Prayer of Reception
2. The **Conditions** to answered prayer and how to fulfill them.
3. How to turn Problems into Opportunities.
4. How to avoid **presumption**.

5. **Devotional** and study ideas.

6. The **Prayer of Commitment**

   Basic principles regarding sickness and health.

In this lesson we will discuss:

1. The meaning of **happiness**.

2. Our role as channels of the **Holy Spirit**.

3. A brief overview of **Intercessory Prayer**.

4. The difference between **hospitality** and **entertaining**.

The Meaning of "Happiness"

We need to answer the following questions before we can formulate a true Christian approach to discipline and helping those who come to us with problems.

1. **What is happiness?**

   Dictionary: "Happiness" is generally defined as a state of well-being and pleasurable satisfaction.

   Bible: There are three words translated as "happy"

   a. To be satisfied.

   b. To be at rest.

   c. To be blessed.

   When people say, "I just want to be happy!" they probably mean, "I am looking for rest, satisfaction, and blessing."

2. **Where is true happiness found?**

   Read **Psalm 16:11** and paraphrase it here: _____

   _____

116

Read **Luke 17:21** and paraphrase it here: _____

_____

    a. When our life is hid in Christ it is filled with peace and rest fullness.

    b. The absence of our Savior in our life is revealed in uneasiness, dissatisfaction and restlessness.

    c. "He who is at peace with God and his fellow man cannot be made miserable."[90]

3. **Why is happiness sought from other sources?**

Read **James 1:14** and paraphrase it here: _____

_____

Because of our own sinful natures, we are drawn into sin. No one makes us sin.

Reflection Thoughts—Who, What or Where is the source of your happiness? Meditate on this question and record your thoughts in your personal journal, or on a **Reflections** page.

Our Role as Channels of the Holy Spirit in Turning People to the True Source of Happiness

Jesus' Example.

1. As our Lord received from the Father, He communicated with us.

Read **John 14:24** and paraphrase it here: _____

_____

Growing in the "YES" of God

Read **Matthew 20:28** and paraphrase it here: _____

_____

2. He lived, thought and prayed for others.

3. Morning by morning He spent time with His Father.

4. Daily He received the anointing of the Holy Spirit.

The Disciples' Instructions

1. The disciples were to follow Christ's example and seek blessings from God and the impartation of the Holy Spirit.

2. They were to work as His representatives.

3. Their faith would be tried and they would be thrown into unexpected positions.

4. They would realize their human insufficiencies and dependence on God to meet the needs of God's children.

5. They needed to receive to impart.

6. They were to turn no one away.

7. God would supply their needs.

How Do We Do It?

1. **Self-distrust**—The most childlike disciple is the most effective and efficient laborer because they become workers together with God, trusting Him for wisdom in every circumstance.

2. **Sanctified and Ready to Minister**—Finally, all of you be of one mind, having compassion for one another; love as brothers, be tenderhearted, be courteous; not returning evil for evil or reviling for reviling, but on the contrary blessing, knowing that you were called to this, that you may inherit a blessing. For He who would love life and see good days, let him refrain his tongue from evil, and his lips from speaking deceit. Let him turn away from evil and do good; let him seek peace and pursue it. For the eyes of the LORD are on the righteous, and His ears are open to their prayers ... But sanctify the Lord God in your hearts, and always be ready to give a defense to everyone who asks you a reason for the hope that is in you, with meekness and fear.—1 Peter 3:8-15.

3. **Unite Our Weakness to His Strength**—One of the chief secrets of failure in Christian work is the refusal of dying to self. Those who feel competent to act without God's counsel are passed by for those who trust all to Him.

Basic Eternal Principles Regarding the Holy Spirit

Only the Influence of the Holy Spirit Can Turn a Man's Mind.

Read **John 16:7-13** and paraphrase it here: _____

_____

_____

_____

Read **John 14:26** and paraphrase it here: _____

_____

The Holy Spirit Works Most Directly Through Christians.

Read **Matthew 5:13-14** and paraphrase it here: _____

_____

Read **Philippians 2:13** and paraphrase it here: _____

_____

Growing in the "YES" of God

We Become Channels of the Holy Spirit by Asking for Him.

Read **Luke 11:13** and paraphrase it here: _____

_____

Read **1 John 5:16** and paraphrase it here: _____

_____

"Christ has **promised** the gift of the Holy Spirit to His church, and the **promise** belongs to us as much as to the first disciples. But like every other **promise** it was given on **conditions**. There are many who believe and profess to claim the Lord's **promise**; they talk about Christ and the Holy Spirit, yet receive no benefit. They do not surrender their soul to be guided and controlled by divine agencies. We cannot use the Holy Spirit. The Spirit is to use us. Through the Spirit, God works in His people *to will and to do of His good pleasure.*—Philippians 2:13. But many will not submit to this. They want to manage themselves. This is why they do not receive the heavenly gift. Only those who wait humbly upon God, who watch for His guidance and grace, is the Spirit given. The power of God awaits their demand and reception. This **promised** blessing, claimed by faith, brings all other blessings in its train. It is given according to the riches of the grace of Christ, and He is ready to supply every soul according to the capacity to receive."[91]

Through Christians, filled with the Holy Spirit, people are to be attracted to the Gospel.

Read **John 6:44** and paraphrase it here: _____

_____

Read **Matthew 5:13-14** and paraphrase them here: _____

_____

People are saved as individuals. If we want to make a difference in someone's life, we must build relationship and come close to them. It is through personal contact and association that we reach others for Him.

"There is eloquence far more powerful than the eloquence of words in the quiet, consistent life of a pure, true Christian."[92]

Work of the Holy Spirit.

We must radiate the kindness and love of God so that people will be attracted to and not repelled from the Gospel. It is not our work to, *convict the world of sin, and of righteousness, and of judgment:*—John 16:8, that is the work of the **Holy Spirit**. The **Holy Spirit** will convince and convert through us. We are to "make people feel comfortable and let the **Holy Spirit** make them feel uncomfortable".

Intercessory Prayer.

Read **James 5:16** and paraphrase it here: _____

_____

Jesus' Prayer —John 17.

The Challenge to Witness.

1. Commune with Christ before communing with men. It takes great wisdom to win souls to Christ and should be preceded by much private prayer.

2. Jesus welcomes the prayers of intercession, pleading for the salvation of His unsaved children.

> **Reflection Thoughts**—What ways do you witness and have you considered being hospitable?

3. God could have saved sinners without our help; but he chose to employ us in the blessing of ministering to others as co-laborers with Him. In order to develop a Christ-like character, we must share in His work. We enter into Christ's joy—the joy of seeing souls come to Christ and embracing His redemptive sacrifice, by participating with Him in this trusted calling.

Hospitality vs. Entertaining

Definitions.

1. Hospitality: The generous reception and gracious disposition to extend friendly treatment to guests.

   Let love be without hypocrisy. Abhor what is evil. Cling to what is good. Be kindly affectionate to one another with brotherly love, in honor giving preference to one another; not lagging in diligence, fervent in spirit, serving the Lord; rejoicing in hope, patient in tribulation, continuing steadfastly in prayer; distributing to the needs of the saints, given to hospitality. Bless those who persecute you; bless and do not curse. Rejoice with those who rejoice, and weep with those who weep. Be of the same mind toward one another. Do not set your mind on high things, but associate with the humble. Do not be wise in your own opinion. Repay no one evil for evil. Have regard for good things in the sight of all men. If it is possible, as much as depends on you, live peaceably with all men. Beloved, do not avenge yourselves, but rather give place to wrath; for it is written, "Vengeance is Mine, I will repay," says the Lord. Therefore, if your enemy is hungry, feed him; if he is thirsty, give him a drink; for in so doing you will heap coals of fire on his head. Do not be overcome by evil, but overcome evil with good.—Romans 12:9-21

2. Entertaining: To amuse, to provide diversions, to receive company, the receiving and accommodating of guests.

Examples

1. Martha

   "Many older brothers and sisters have an irritating tendency to take charge, a habit developed while growing up. We can easily see this pattern in Martha, the older sister of Mary and Lazarus. She was used to being in control.

"The fact that Martha, Mary and Lazarus are remembered for their hospitality takes on added significance when we note that hospitality was a social requirement in Jewish culture at the time. It was considered shameful to turn anyone away from your door. Apparently this family did very well at this practice.

"Martha worried about details. She wished to please, to serve, to do the right thing—but she often succeeded in making everyone around her uncomfortable. Perhaps as the oldest, she felt the fear of shame if her home did not measure up to expectations. She tried to do everything she could to make sure that wouldn't happen. As a result, she found it hard to relax and enjoy her guests. She found it even harder to accept Mary's lack of cooperation in all the preparations. Her feelings were so intense that she finally asked Jesus to settle the matter. He gently corrected her attitude and showed her that while her priorities were good, they were not the best. The attention she gave to her guest should be more important than what she tried to do for them."[93]

We should not let our gift of hospitality or serving become self-serving or degenerate to busy work.

2. Mary

"Hospitality is an art. Making sure a guest is welcomed, warmed and well-fed requires creativity, organization, and teamwork. Their ability to accomplish this makes Mary and her sister Martha one of the best hospitality teams in the *Bible*. Their frequent guest was Jesus.

"For Mary, hospitality meant giving more attention to the guest Himself than to the needs He might have. She would rather talk than cook. She was more interested in her guest's word than in the cleanliness of her home or the timeliness of her meals. She let her older sister Martha take care of those details. Mary's approach to events shows her to be mainly a "responder." She did little preparation—her role was participation. Unlike her sister, who had to learn to stop and listen, Mary needed to learn that action is often appropriate and necessary.

"We first meet Mary during a visit Jesus paid to her home. She simply sat at His feet and listened. When Martha became irritated at her sister's lack of help, Jesus stated that Mary's choice to enjoy His company was the most appropriate response at the time."[94]

Reflection Thoughts—What kind of hospitality does Jesus receive in your life? Are you so busy planning and running your life that you neglect precious time with Him? Or do you respond to Him by listening to His word, then finding ways to worship Him with your life? That is the kind of hospitality He longs for from each of us.

Assignment

1. Pray the following prayers from the **Daily Prayer Sheet**

   For Forgiveness

   Dear Heavenly Father,

   I **ask** that You will forgive me for _____;

   I **believe** that You have forgiven me because You have promised in 1 John 1:9;

   I **thank** You that You have forgiven me.

   In Jesus' name, Amen.

   For Intercession and Soul Winning

   Dear Heavenly Father,

   I **ask** that You will give me life to give _____;

   I **believe** that You are giving me life to give him/her because You have promised in 1 John 5:16;

   I **thank** You that You have given me life to give him/her.

   In Jesus' name, Amen.

   For the Holy Spirit

   Dear Heavenly Father,

   I **ask** that You will give me the Holy Spirit;

   I **believe** that You are giving me the Holy Spirit because You have promised in Luke 11:13;

   I **thank** You that You have given me the Holy Spirit.

   In Jesus' name, Amen.

2. *Bible* Promises about the Holy Spirit

   Find five *Bible* **promises** about the **Holy Spirit** that you could use for yourself or share with a friend. Remember to record these **promises** on your **Record of Experiences** and how they apply to the personal problems in your life at this time.

3. Journal on a **Reflections** page

Using your own personal journal or a **Reflections** page, record who, and how, you are interceding for this week. In addition, journal what those did this week's lesson provoke?

Record of Experiences

Record of Experiences

This record of experiences will help you keep a list of the problems you had, the promises you claimed and the date your prayers were answered. It will help to increase your faith in the future when you can look back and see how God so miraculously intervened.

Date Asked	Problem	Promise Text	Date Answered	How Answered

Growing in the "YES" of God

Speak Lord, Your servant is listening—1 Samuel 3:9-10 NIV

Weekly Reflections

_____

_____

_____

_____

_____

_____

_____

_____

_____

_____

_____

"Here I am, send me, I'm available Lord."

—*Praying in the "YES" of God,* p. 170

LESSON EIGHT—LIVING FOR SERVICE

Always be prepared to give an answer to everyone who asks you to give the reason for the hope that you have.
                                        —1 Peter 3:15

*(Please refer to pages 163-173 in **Living Volume One: Praying in the "YES" of God** while you are studying this chapter.)*

Introduction

What we have studied so far:

1. The **Prayer of Reception**.
2. The conditions to answered prayer and how to fulfill them.
3. How to turn problems into opportunities.
4. How to avoid presumption.
5. Devotional and study ideas.

Growing in the "YES" of God

6. The **Prayer of Commitment**.

   Basic principles regarding sickness and health.

7. The Holy Spirit.

   a. The meaning of happiness.

   b. Our role as channels of the Holy Spirit.

   c. A brief overview of Intercessory Prayer.

   d. The difference between hospitality and entertaining.

In this lesson we will learn:

The science and challenge of Christian witnessing and soul-winning.

We are to do our part in reaching the world by staying close to God as His co-laborers—His disciples. We are His hands, working in cooperation with Him, to reach out to the distressed, to cheer the sorrowing, to bring the broken to Jesus. We are to desire and live out His attributes by Christ abiding in us.

The Science of Christian Witnessing and Soul-Winning

THE FOUR "I'S" OF AUTHENTIC WITNESS

1. Identification

2. Involvement

3. Intercession

4. Incisiveness

Becoming "all things to all people" does not mean compromising our beliefs. Rather, it implies that we should use all our previous experiences to identify with people who need Christ. Often, the things we've been through, learned, achieved, or attained by the Lord's grace give us a point of contact. Christ will use everything we've been through in both successes and failures to make a difference for the Kingdom when we are surrendered to His will.

A Sevenfold Approach of Christian Witnessing and Soul-winning

"Authentic witnessing requires a gospel that is personally and passionately ours."[95]

1. **Jesus**

   a. "The way from God to a human heart is through a human heart."—S.D. Gordon. What comes out of our mouths is dependent on what's in our hearts. We can speak no more than we've allowed the Lord to impute to our hearts. Jesus promises us that out of our hearts will flow rivers of living water—the Holy Spirit. When we allow the Spirit to live in us, He will speak through us. Our words take on power and love which we cannot produce by ourselves. If we lack warmth and affirmation for people, the trouble is probably in our hearts. When we invite the Holy Spirit to dwell in us, we are given the gift of wise speech.

   b. We can use words to deny our Lord. Often we do it in what we refuse to say as much as by what we say. When we have an opportunity to witness but remain silent, that's denial. Or think of the ways we contradict what we believe by the way we talk. The very fact that we talk so little about what we believe gives the impression that we believe very little. There's more than one way of saying, "I do not know the Man!"

   c. Often people say, "My witness is my life. I don't talk with others about my faith." That is making quite a claim for our life! But it is also a denial of people's right to know what is behind our quality of life.

   d. Tell them how you found Jesus, and how blessed you have been since you gained an experience in His service. Tell them what blessing comes to you as you sit at the feet of Jesus, and learn precious lessons from His word. We find our "center" when we fix our eyes on Jesus.

> **Reflection Thoughts**—I Peter 3:15 tells us to *"be ready always to give an answer to everyone who asks you to give the reason for the hope that you have"*. This week, prepare an elevator talk – what can you say in a few minutes to plant seeds of faith and hope in Jesus by your testimony. Write it down in your journal or on your reflection page and memorize it so you are prepared to share it in a moment's notice.

2. **Joy—Express the joy that comes from the Christian life**

Read **Nehemiah 8:10** and paraphrase it here: _____

_____

_____

a. Tell them of the joy in living a Christian life. To honor Jesus is to become like Him and to work for Him. This should be our life's highest ambition and its greatest joy.

b. Equate Jesus with joy.

   Read **Psalm 16:11** and paraphrase it here: _____

   _____

   _____

   Read **Psalm 22:3** and paraphrase it here: _____

   _____

   _____

c. "God is love; God is fire. The two are one. The Holy Spirit baptizes with fire. Spirit-filled souls are ablaze for God. They love with a love which glows. They believe with a faith that kindles. They serve with a devotion that consumes. They hate sin with a fierceness that burns. They rejoice with a joy that radiates. Love is perfected in the fire of God."—Samuel Chadwick

> **Reflection Thoughts**—Consider Joy and Happiness. In your mind, what defines each? Where does your joy come from? Can you define it for someone seeking to know about this joy you possess?

3. **Faith—Express faith and confidence in them**

Read **John 1:47** and paraphrase it here: _____

_____

   a. Jesus honored man by putting His confidence in them and showing trust. If we are one in Christ Jesus, we will place His estimate upon every human being. We will be encouraging and supportive, offering sympathy and confidence.

   b. If there is authenticity in our life and words, they will be more prone to listen to what Jesus can do for them. We can build trust, or break it down by negative talk, criticism, or gossip. Our witness will become tarnished, and we will not be the people others will trust with their deepest concerns. We are accountable for how we use our words.

   c. The Lord has arranged relationships for all of us with people He wants to love through us. Our expressions of love by words and explanations of what He means to us, and can mean to them, could be life changing for them.

> **Reflection Thoughts**—How do you convey faith in others? Have you grown in your ability to trust others and seek to live your life in a way that other's can trust you with their deepest issues?

4. **Hope—Inspire hope through acceptance and encouragement**

   a. *We are saved by hope.*—Romans 8:24 KJV. Jesus treated even the lowest with respect. He honored man. We must help all to know that it is not too late for them. We must never express any shock at anything someone trusts sharing with us. We will deem all men our brothers if we have allowed the Holy Spirit access to us. We all have similar temptations and trials, often falling and struggling to get back on our feet, fighting discouragement, anxious for a word of support and sympathy. We are to awaken hope in their hearts.

   b. True friends will counsel, and impart "magnetic hopefulness" and uplifting faith.

c. We can say with certainty to anyone: "I believe God has a special purpose for you, a particular work" or something similar, because God has a destiny for each of us to fill for the Kingdom that no one else can fill.

Reflection Thoughts—Do you live your life as a witness of hope that is in you? If you are hopeful, you can share hope, how will you do that?

---

5. **Love—Demonstrate your love for them**

a. We are influential people. Every day we are influencing the people around us about what it means to live for Christ. If the people of our lives had to write a definition of Christianity from what they see and hear from us, what would they write? Our influence is either positive or negative. People are reading the signals all the time.

b. People and their needs are our agenda. Our faith is to "pack a wallop" for others. Everything Jesus gives us is for our outreach and impact on others. When we settle that, life becomes blessed indeed. We were meant to have impact, influence, and inspiration in the lives of the people we touch. What stands in the way of people seeing Christ's light burning in us? For some, it's our personalities, which need Christ's transformation; for others it's privatism, which keeps us from sharing our faith; for still others, it is simply lack of loving concern. The Psalmist reminds us of our calling in Psalm 107:2.

Look up **Psalm 107:2** and paraphrase it here: _____

_____

c. Christ is ready to use us wherever we are.

d. What the Lord requires, He inspires. We are to be channels of His love. Our challenge is to allow Him to love us so that we can love others. That's the exciting adventure of being a Christian!

e. *Love is patient and kind; love is not jealous or boastful; it is not arrogant or rude. Love does not insist on its own way; it is not irritable or resentful; it does not rejoice at wrong, but rejoices in the right.—*1 Corinthians 13:4-6 RSV.

f. *By this we know love that He laid down His life for us; and we ought to lay down our lives for the brethren. But if any one has the world's goods and sees his brother in need, yet closes his heart against him, how does God's love abide in him? Little children, let us not love in word or speech but in deed and in truth.—1 John 3:16-18 RSV.*

g. The Law of Kindness should be upon our lips and grace in our hearts. There should be no sharp, critical, blunt or harsh words spoken.

Look up **Proverbs 15:1** and paraphrase it here: _____

_____

_____

h. Let the smile on the face show love. Let the warm handshake reflect fellowship. Let every comment be filled with confidence and love.

Reflection Thought—Christ Is Love. What is your definition of love? How do you demonstrate Christ's love for others in your life? What do you need to work on in this area of your life? Are there particular people that you struggle to love? Pray and ask God for wisdom and guidance on how to approach these people with loving heart and mind.

---

6. **Choice—Recognize their right to choose**

a. *And if you be unwilling to serve the LORD, choose this day whom you will serve, whether the gods your fathers served ... or the gods of the Amorites ... but as for me and my house, we will serve the LORD.—*Joshua 24:15 RSV.

b. "Arbitrary words and actions stir up the worst passions of the human heart."[96]

c. We can say, "I do not have the right to make a decision for you." or "It is not my place to tell you what to do."

Growing in the "YES" of God

> **Reflection Thoughts**—Do you recognize that there are some that may not be open to your witnessing? Do you recognize each individual has the right to choose or not to choose... and not just in spiritual issues, but in life in general? Do you allow others around you to make their own choices, and face the consequences – whether good or bad, or do you try to control, dictate, and/or manipulate to have them do what you deem best? How does that make you feel when others don't bend to your will? This week validate your confidence in someone else by respecting their choices.

7. **Humility—Be humble**

Read **Philippians 2:3-8** and paraphrase it here: _____

_____

_____

a. With all of our weaknesses and inadequacies how can we communicate the faith? _____

_____

_____

_____

b. Imitate God's grace and forgiveness. How you handle your failures is an invaluable part of your witness. It's not how **great** we are, but how **great** God has been in our life. We can say something like, "I've probably made two mistakes for every one you have made."

> **Reflection Thoughts**—What does this quote mean to you, "Lord, make me so humble, I don't know that I am".—Andrew Murray. Journal your thoughts.

The Keys of Heaven

Read **Matthew 16:13-20** and paraphrase them here: _____

_____

_____

_____

_____

Read **Isaiah 33:6** and paraphrase it here: _____

_____

If we only trusted ourselves as much as Jesus does! What exceptional things could happen if we relinquished our own negative view of ourselves and saw ourselves as Jesus sees us. We are His children.

> **Reflection Thoughts**—What negative self-talk keeps you from moving forward to share Jesus with others? Where do you think this "talk" comes from? Pray and ask God for clarity of your thoughts in your worth in Him.

When we refuse to share, we lock the door to someone else He desires to reach through us. There are keys to soul-winning. A full key ring can unlock the varied, different doors for each kind of person we meet. A full key ring might include:

1. The key of listening (if in person, eye contact, not distracted attention)
2. The key of caring with compassion

3. The key of discussion- with felt acceptance of the person not necessarily their view point

4. The key of witness lived out and spoken

5. The key of prayer for another with faithful intercession

6. The key of unchanging, unconditional love exemplified (source unknown)

7. The key of forgiveness

We have been given power to forgive in His name and to assure people of His love. What a trust. What an opportunity!

Love is involvement. **"STARS"** reminds us how:

Sacrifice of time, energy and means, **out of**

Thoughtfulness and caring, **promotes**

Acceptance from a heart that **promises**

Respect of privacy (no gossip); all of which should be **incorprated in**

Service for God and our fellow man.

The Christian is filled with tremendous vitality because he knows without question that he is **loved**, **forgiven**, **cherished** and **empowered**. Jesus called His disciples to out-**love** and out-serve the whole world.

If we don't believe that what's happened to us in our relationship to Christ ought to happen to everyone, then probably too little has happened to us … If we are not so excited about what we have found that we want everyone to experience it, then we have not found very much. Consider that some people you encounter may make a decision about Christ by what they see of Him in you. Will they take Christ seriously because of what they see that He has done for you? Have you found an exciting, adventuresome faith that you want everyone to have? Who would want to know Christ because of what they see in you?

And let us not be weary in well doing; for in due season we shall reap, if we faint not.—Galatians 6:9

Assignment

1. Pray the prayers from the **Daily Prayer Sheet**

   For Forgiveness

   Dear Heavenly Father,

   I **ask** that You will forgive me for _____;

   I **believe** that You have forgiven me because You have promised in 1 John 1:9;

   I **thank** You that You have forgiven me.

   In Jesus' name, Amen.

   For Intercession and Soul Winning

   Dear Heavenly Father,

   I **ask** that You will give me life to give _____;

   I **believe** that You are giving me life to give him/her because You have promised in 1 John 5:16;

   I **thank** You that You have given me life to give him/her.

   In Jesus' name, Amen.

   For the Holy Spirit

   Dear Heavenly Father,

   I **ask** that You will give me the Holy Spirit;

   I **believe** that You are giving me the Holy Spirit because You have promised in Luke 11:13;

   I **thank** You that You have given me the Holy Spirit.

   In Jesus' name, Amen.

2. *Bible* Promises that speak of **joy** and **peace**

   Find five *Bible* promises that speak to you of **joy** and **peace** that you could use in witnessing to someone. Using the **Record of Experience** record the Scriptures that the Holy Spirit reveals to you and how they apply to the way you face life and how they will help you deal with your present personal problems.

3. Journal on a **Reflections** page

   Using your own personal journal or a **Reflections** page, record your thoughts on the following question:

   If you were paid $10.00 an hour for consciously working at loving others, how much money would you have made this past week? How much will you earn this week?

4. Read *An Illustration of His Methods* on the following pages; journal your thoughts.

5. So far in this course, we have learned how to pray the **Prayer of Reception**, which is part of the **Prayer of Faith**, and have been greatly blessed as we have claimed the promises of God and received His gifts. *Blessings are enjoyed best when they are shared with others.*

   Seek to teach someone this week how to claim *Bible* **promises** by putting into practice the following information. Journal your experience.

   The following suggested procedure has been used successfully in teaching others how to pray the **Prayer of Reception**.

   You may either copy the next page or go to our website: **www.FreedomInSurrender.net/Resources** for a single-page copy of these directions to print and take with you.

Directions for Teaching how to Claim Promises

Follow the Sevenfold Approach to Christian Witnessing and Counseling in this lesson, particularly inspiring hope through acceptance and encouragement. This will be of special help in case there is any mental depression in the person you share with.

1. Tell experiences of your own or ones you have read or heard regarding answers to Receptive Prayer.

2. While you are opening the *Bible* to John 14:26, invite the counselee to kneel with you to claim the promise for the Holy Spirit "to teach you all things."

3. After this prayer, place a piece of paper and a pencil in the hands of the counselee.

4. Go over all conditions to claiming promises and the recommended procedure. Use the *Bible* as a textbook and have the counselee write the conditions down.

5. Claim a promise that is the solution to their problem with *Bible* open and finger on the text. (If you have difficulty finding a promise relating to the problem, claim the promise for wisdom in James 1:5, and use a concordance and other reference sources to find it.)

6. Rise from your knees and express "magnetic hopefulness" that they now have the answer to their problem and they will recognize it when they need it most.

7. Remind them that they should claim this promise 2-3 times a day.

8. Wait about two or three days, or as the Spirit leads, and then go to see them and hear of their wonderful experiences.

9. Encourage them at the end of your latest visit to attend a class you will start and share their experiences. Assure them they will gain more knowledge about claiming *Bible* promises. Tell them you have just given them a start on the road to the most rewarding experience they can ever have ...**Living** and **Growing in the "YES" of God**.

An Illustration of His Methods

The most complete illustration of Christ's methods as a teacher is found in His training of the first disciples. Upon these twelve men were to rest weighty responsibilities. He had chosen them as men whom He could imbue with His Spirit, and who could be fitted to carry forward His work on earth when He should leave it. To them, above all others, He gave the advantage of His own companionship. Through personal association He impressed Himself upon these chosen co-laborers. *The life was manifested,* says John the beloved, *and we have seen, and bear witness.*—1 John 1:2 KJV.

Only by the communion of mind with mind and heart with heart, of the human with the divine, can be communicated that vitalizing energy which it is the work of true education to impart.

In the training of His disciples the Savior followed the system of education established at the beginning. The Twelve, with a few others who ministered to their needs and were from time to time connected with them, formed the family of Jesus. They accompanied Him on His journeys, shared His trials and hardships, and, as much as possible, entered into His work.

Sometimes He taught them as they sat together on the mountainside, sometimes beside the sea or from the fisherman's boat, sometimes as they walked together. Whenever He spoke to the multitude, the disciples formed the inner circle. They pressed close beside Him that they might lose nothing of His instruction. They were attentive listeners, eager to understand the truths they were to teach in all lands and to all ages.

The first pupils of Jesus were chosen from the ranks of the common people. They were humble, unlettered fishermen unschooled in the learning and customs of the rabbis, but trained by the stern discipline of toil and hardship. They had native ability and a teachable spirit. They could be instructed and molded for the Savior's work. In the common walks of life there are many workers patiently treading the round of their daily tasks, unconscious of latent powers that, if roused to action, would place them among the world's great leaders. Such were those who were called by the Savior to be His co-laborers. And they had the advantage of three years' training by the greatest educator this world has ever known.

In these first disciples there was marked diversity. Destined to be the world's teachers, they represented widely varied types of character. There were Levi Matthew the publican, called from a life of business and subservience to Rome; Simon the zealot, an uncompromising foe of the imperial authority; warmhearted Peter, impulsive and self-sufficient, with Andrew his brother; Judas the Judean, polished, capable, and mean-spirited; Philip and Thomas, faithful and earnest yet slow of heart to believe; James the less and Jude, of less prominence among the group but men of force, positive both in their faults and in their virtues; Nathanael, a child in sincerity and trust; and the ambitious, loving-hearted sons of Zebedee.

In order to carry forward their work successfully, these disciples, differing widely in natural characteristics, in training, and in habits of life, needed to come into unity of feeling, thought, and action. To secure this unity, Christ worked to bring them into unity with Himself. The burden of His efforts for them is expressed in His prayer to the Father, *that they all may be one; as You, Father, are in Me, and I in You, that they also may be one in Us: ... that the world may know that You have sent Me, and have loved them, as You have loved Me.*—John 17:21-23.

The Transforming Power of Christ

Of the twelve disciples, four were to act a leading part, each in a distinct way. In preparation for this, Christ taught them, foreseeing all: James, destined to swift death by the sword; John, who followed his Master the longest in labor and persecution; Peter, the pioneer in teaching the heathen world; and Judas, in service more capable than his associates, yet brooding in his soul—these were the objects of Christ's greatest solicitude and the ones who received His most frequent and careful instruction.

Peter, James, and John sought every opportunity to come into close contact with their Master, and their desire was granted. Of all the Twelve their relationship to Him was closest. John could be satisfied only with a still closer intimacy, and this he obtained. At that first conference beside the Jordan, when Andrew, having heard Jesus, hurried away to call his brother, John sat silent, rapt in the contemplation of wondrous themes. He followed the Savior, ever an eager, absorbed listener.

Yet John's character was not faultless. He and his brother were called *Sons of thunder.*—Mark 3:17. John was proud, ambitious, and combative, but beneath all this the divine Teacher discerned a sincere, loving heart. Jesus rebuked his self-seeking, disappointed his ambitions, and tested his faith, but He revealed to him that for which his soul longed—the beauty of holiness, His own transforming love. To His Father He said, *I have manifested Thy name to the men whom Thou gavest Me out of the world;*—John 17:6 RSV.

John's was a nature that longed for love, sympathy, and companionship. As a flower drinks in the sun and dew, so he drank in the divine light and life. In adoration and love he beheld the Savior, until his character reflected the character of his Master. *Behold*, he said, *what manner of love the Father has bestowed on us, that we should be called children of God.*—1 John 3:1.

From Weakness to Strength

The history of none of the disciples better illustrates Christ's method of training than does the history of Peter. Bold, aggressive, and self-confident, Peter often erred and often received reproof, yet his warmhearted loyalty and devotion to Christ were recognized and commended. Patiently and lovingly the Savior dealt with His impetuous disciple, seeking to check his self-confidence, and to teach him humility, obedience, and trust. But only in part was the lesson learned. Self-assurance was not uprooted.

Often Jesus attempted to open to the disciples the scenes of His trial and suffering, but the knowledge was unwelcome, and they did not see. Self-pity, which shrank from fellowship with Christ in suffering, prompted Peter's protest, *Far be it from You, Lord; this shall not happen to You!*—Matthew 16:22. His words expressed the thought and feeling of the Twelve.

So they went on, the crisis drawing nearer. They were boastful and contentious, hoping for high positions, and not dreaming of the cross.

Peter's experience in betraying Jesus had a lesson for them all. To self-trust, trial is defeat. Christ could not prevent the sure outcome of unforsaken evil, but as His hand had been outstretched to save when the waves were about to sweep over Peter, so did His love reach out for his rescue when the deep waters swept over his soul. Again and again, on the very verge of ruin, Peter's words of boasting brought him nearer and still nearer to the brink. Over and over again was given the warning, *You will deny three times that you know Me.*—Luke 22:34. But the grieved, loving heart of the disciple responded, *Lord, I am ready to go with You, both to prison, and to death.*—Luke 22:33. And He who reads the heart gave to Peter the message, little valued then, but that in the swift-falling darkness would shed a ray of hope: *Simon, Simon! Indeed, Satan has asked for you, that he may sift you as wheat. But I have prayed for you, that your faith should not fail: and when you have returned to Me, strengthen your brethren.*—Luke 22:31-32.

When in the judgment hall the words of denial had been spoken; when Peter's love and loyalty, awakened under the Savior's glance of pity, love, and sorrow, had sent him forth to the garden where Christ had wept and prayed; when his tears of remorse dropped on the ground—then the Savior's words were an anchor for his soul. Christ, though foreseeing his sin, had not abandoned him to despair.

If the look that Jesus directed toward him had spoken condemnation instead of pity, how dense would have been the darkness that encompassed Peter, how reckless the despair of his tortured soul! In that hour of anguish and self-abhorrence, what could have held him back from the path trodden by Judas?

He who could not spare His disciple the anguish, did not leave him alone to its bitterness. His is a love that never fails nor forsakes.

Human beings, themselves given to evil, cannot read the heart; they do not know its struggle and pain. They need to learn of the rebuke that is love, of the blow that wounds to heal, of the warning that speaks hope.

It was not John, the one who watched with Jesus in the judgment hall, the one who stood beside His cross, and who of the Twelve was first at the tomb—it was not John, but Peter, who was mentioned by Christ after His resurrection. *Tell His disciples—and Peter*, the angel said, *that He is going before you into Galilee; there you will see Him.*—Mark 16:7.

At the last meeting of Christ with the disciples by the sea, Peter, tested three times by the question, "Do you love Me?" was restored to his place among the Twelve. His work was appointed him; he was to feed the Lord's flock. Then, as His last personal direction, Jesus said, *You follow Me.*—John 21:17, 22. Now he could appreciate the words. Knowing more fully both his own weakness and Christ's power, he was ready to trust and obey. In His strength he could follow his Master.

Growing in the "YES" of God

At the close of his ministry, the disciple once so unready to discern the cross counted it a joy to yield up his life for the gospel, feeling only that to die in the same manner as his Master died was too great an honor.

Peter's transformation was a miracle of divine tenderness. It is a life lesson to all who desire to follow in the steps of the Master Teacher.

A Lesson in Love

Jesus warned, cautioned, and reproved His disciples, but neither John, Peter, nor the other disciples left Him. Notwithstanding the reproofs, they chose to be with Jesus. And the Savior did not, because of their errors, withdraw from them. If they will be disciplined and taught by Jesus, He takes men and women as they are, with all their faults and weaknesses, and trains them for His service.

But there was one of the Twelve to whom Christ spoke no word of direct reproof until very near the close of His work.

Judas introduced an element of antagonism among the disciples. In connecting with Jesus he had responded to the attraction of His character and life. He had sincerely desired a change in himself, and had hoped to experience this through being with Jesus. But this desire did not become predominant. He was ruled by the hope of selfish benefit in the worldly kingdom that he expected Christ to establish. Though recognizing the divine power of the love of Christ, Judas continued to cherish his own judgment, opinions, and his disposition to criticize and condemn. Christ's motives and movements, often so far above his comprehension, excited doubt and disapproval, and his own questionings and ambitions were insinuated to the disciples. Many of their contentions for supremacy, and much of their dissatisfaction with Christ's methods, originated with Judas.

Jesus, seeing that to antagonize was but to harden, refrained from direct conflict. Christ endeavored to heal the narrowing selfishness of Judas' life through contact with His own self-sacrificing love. In His teaching He unfolded principles that struck at the root of the disciple's self-centered ambitions. Lesson after lesson was thus given, and many a time Judas realized that his character had been portrayed and his sin pointed out, but he would not yield.

Mercy's pleading having been resisted, the impulse of evil bore final sway. Angered at an implied rebuke and made desperate by the disappointment of his ambitious dreams, Judas surrendered his soul to the demon of greed and determined to betray his Master. From the Passover chamber and the joy of Christ's presence he went forth to his evil work.

Jesus knew from the beginning who they were who did not believe, and who would betray Him.—John 6:64. Yet, knowing all, He had withheld no pleading of mercy or gift of love.

Seeing his danger, Christ had brought Judas close to Himself, within the inner circle of His chosen and trusted disciples. Day after day, when the burden lay heaviest upon His own heart, He had borne the pain of continual contact with that stubborn, suspicious, brooding spirit. He had witnessed and labored to counteract among His disciples that continuous, secret, subtle antagonism. And all this that no possible saving influence might be lacking to that imperiled soul!

So far as Judas himself was concerned, Christ's work of love had been to no avail. But to the other disciples it ever would be an example of tenderness and longsuffering as they dealt with the tempted and erring. And it had other lessons. At the ordination of the Twelve, the disciples had greatly desired that Judas should become one of their number. He had come more into contact with the world than they, he was a man of discernment and executive ability, and, having a high estimate of his own qualifications, he had led the disciples to hold him in the same regard. But the methods he wanted to introduce into Christ's work were based on principles aimed to achieve worldly recognition and honor. The working out of these desires in the life of Judas helped the disciples to understand the antagonism between the principle of self-aggrandizement and Christ's principle of humility and self-sacrifice. In the fate of Judas they saw the end to which self-serving tends.

For these disciples the mission of Christ finally accomplished its purpose. Little by little His example and lessons of self-denial molded their characters. His death destroyed their hope of worldly greatness. The fall of Peter, the apostasy of Judas, their own failure in forsaking Christ in His anguish and peril, swept away their self-sufficiency. As they saw their own weakness and something of the greatness of the work committed to them, they felt their need of their Master's guidance at every step.

Growing in the "YES" of God

Many of His lessons, when spoken, they had not appreciated or under-stood; now they longed to recall these lessons, to hear again His words. With what joy His assurance now came back to them: *The Helper ... whom the Father will send in My name, He will teach you all things, and bring to your remembrance all things that I said to you.*—John 14:26.

The disciples had seen Christ ascend from the Mount of Olives. And as the heavens received Him, there had come back to them His parting promise, *and lo, I am with you always, even to the end of the age.*—Matthew 28:20. They knew that His sympathies were still with them. They knew that they had a representative, an advocate, at the throne of God. In the name of Jesus they presented their petitions, repeating His promise, *Whatever you ask the Father in My name, He will give you.*—John 16:23.

Faithful to His promise, the Divine One, exalted in the heavenly courts, imparted of His fullness to His followers on earth. His enthronement at God's right hand was signaled by the outpouring of the Holy Spirit on His disciples. By the work of Christ these disciples had been led to feel their need of the Spirit, and under the Spirit's teaching they received their final preparation and went forth to their lifework.

No longer were they ignorant and uncultured. No longer were they a col-lection of independent units or discordant and conflicting elements. No longer were their hopes set on worldly greatness. They were of *one accord*, of one mind and one soul. Christ filled their thoughts. The advancement of His kingdom was their aim. In mind and character they had become like their Master, and people *realized that they had been with Jesus.*—Acts 4:13.

Then there was such a revelation of the glory of Christ as never before had been witnessed by mortals. Through the cooperation of the divine Spirit the labors of the humble men whom Christ had chosen stirred the world. In a single generation the gospel was carried to every nation under heaven.

The presence of the same Spirit that instructed the disciples of old will produce the same results in educational work today. This is the end to which true education tends. This is the work that God designs it to ac-complish.[97]

Record of Experiences

Record of Experiences

This record of experiences will help you keep a list of the problems you had, the promises you claimed and the date your prayers were answered. It will help to increase your faith in the future when you can look back and see how God so miraculously intervened.

Date Asked	Problem	Promise Text	Date Answered	How Answered

Speak Lord, Your servant is listening—1 Samuel 3:9-10 NIV

Weekly Reflections

_____

_____

_____

_____

_____

_____

_____

_____

_____

_____

_____

_____

"You can get so close to God that nothing can hurt you."
—*Praying in the "YES" of God*, p, 148

Lesson Nine—How to Have Peace of Mind

Have no anxiety about anything, but in everything by prayer and supplication with thanksgiving let your requests be made known to God. And the peace of God, which passes all understanding, will keep your hearts and your minds in Christ Jesus.
—Philippians 4:6-7 RSV

*(Please refer to pages 68-73 in **Living Volume One: Praying in the "YES" of God** while you are studying this chapter.)*

Introduction

What we have studied so far:

1. The **Prayer of Reception**
2. The **Conditions** to answered **prayer** and how to fulfill them.

Growing in the "YES" of God

3. How to turn Problems into Opportunities.

4. How to avoid **presumption**.

5. **Devotional** and study ideas.

6. The **Prayer of Commitment**

   Basic principles regarding sickness and health.

7. The Holy Spirit

   a. The meaning of **happiness**.

   b. Our role as channels of the **Holy Spirit**.

   c. A brief overview of **Intercessory Prayer**.

   d. The difference between **hospitality** and **entertaining**.

8. The science and challenge of **Christian witnessing** and **soul-winning**.

In this lesson we will learn:

1. How to have **peace of mind**.

   a. Christ's example regarding **peace of mind**.

   b. The study of the spiritual principles involved in receiving and maintaining **peace of mind**.

2. As we incorporate God's promises in our **prayer** life, we draw from Him **peace**, comfort and hope that will develop fruits of **peace**, **joy** and **faith**. As we bring these **promises** into our own life, we bring them into the lives of others.

Christ's Example

1. Christ had peace of mind under all circumstances and experiences of life. "Christ never murmured, never uttered discontent, displeasure, or resentment. He was never disheartened, discouraged ruffled, or fretted. He was patient, calm, and self-possessed under the most exciting and trying circumstances."[98]

2. We can have the identical experience by faith in Him.

   Read **Isaiah 26:3** and paraphrase it here:_____

   _____

152

Read **John 14:27** and paraphrase it here: _____

_____

    a. "Christ bore the test of character in our behalf that we might bear this test in our own behalf through the divine strength He has brought to us."[99]

    b. "He who is at peace with God and his fellow men cannot be made miserable."[100]

Praise brings a positive attitude. "Do not dishonor God by words of repining, but praise Him with heart and soul and voice. Look on the bright side of everything. Do not bring a cloud or shadow into your home. Praise Him who is the light of your countenance and your God. Do this, and see how smoothly everything will go." [101] "If you will seek the Lord and be converted every day; if you will of your own spiritual choice be free and joyous in God if with gladsome consent of heart to His gracious call you come wearing the yoke of Christ,—the yoke of obedience and service,—all your murmurings will be stilled, all your difficulties will be removed, all the perplexing problems that now confront you will be solved."[102]

How to Have Peace of Mind

Read **Philippians 4:4-9.** Enumerate the points in this passage.

1. _____

2. _____

3. _____

_____

_____

_____

4. _____

_____

_____

5. _____

_____

Read **John 16:33** and paraphrase it here: _____

_____

_____

The Conditions of Receiving Peace of Mind

1. **Rejoice Always**.

    Read **Philippians 4:4** and paraphrase it here: _____

    _____

    Read **James 1:2-5** and paraphrase them here: _____

    _____

    _____

    _____

Read **Romans 5:1-4** and paraphrase them here: _____

_____

_____

_____

"The fact that we are called upon to endure trial shows that the Lord Jesus sees in us something precious which He desires to develop."[103] "It will make an infinite difference with you whether trials shall prove your faith to be genuine, or show that your prayers are only a form."[104]

2. **Have a yielding spirit.**

Read **Philippians 4:5** and paraphrase it here: _____

_____

Read **Mark 9:35** and paraphrase it here: _____

_____

"The kingdom of Satan is a kingdom of force; every individual regards every other as an obstacle in the way of his own advancement, or a steppingstone on which he himself may climb to a higher place ... The simplicity, the self-forgetfulness, and the confiding love as of a little child are the tributes that Heaven values. These are the characteristics of real greatness"[105]

3. **Present your case to God and claim His promises.**

Read **Philippians 4:6** and paraphrase it here: _____

_____

"When perplexities arise, and difficulties confront you, look not to humanity for help. Trust all with God."[106]

4. **Accept the peace of mind God is willing to give us.**

And the peace of God, which transcends human understanding, will keep constant guard over your hearts and minds as they rest in Christ Jesus."—Philippians 4:7

The Conditions of Maintaining Peace of Mind

1. **Meditate only on positive things**.

Read **Philippians 4:8** and paraphrase it here: _____

_____

"It is a law of the mind that it gradually adapts itself to the subjects upon which it is trained to dwell."[107]

"It is a law both of the intellectual and the spiritual nature, that by beholding we become changed."[108] We should commit the promises of God to memory and make them our own. Then when unexpected trials or temptations enter our life, we will be forearmed and fortified. We must hide God's word in our hearts in order for the Holy Spirit to bring it to our remembrance.

Read **Psalm 119:11** and paraphrase it here: _____

_____

"It is a law of nature that our thoughts, and feelings are encouraged and strengthened as we give them utterance."[109]

a. Words express our thoughts and thoughts also follow words. We should give more expression to our faith and our love and appreciation for God, rejoicing in the blessings He has given us and lifting our voices in praise.

b. "If you do not feel lighthearted and joyous do not talk of your feelings ... Instead of thinking of your discouragements, think of the power you can claim in Christ's name. Let your thoughts be directed to the evidences of the great love of God's for you. Faith can endure trials, resist temptations, bear up under disappointment."[110]

c. "It is not wise to look to ourselves and study our emotions. If we do this, the enemy will present difficulties and temptations that weaken faith and destroy courage. Closely to study our emotions and give way to our feelings is to entertain doubt and entangle ourselves in perplexity. We are to look away from self to Jesus."[111]

d. Think on the power of Jesus that is available to us through the promises.

e. If we contemplate the faults of others, we will become skillful faultfinders and our peace of mind will be destroyed. We choose to be negative or positive.

f. We can become positive Christians by following the principle of Philippians 4:8.

g. Praise and looking on the bright side of everything brings a positive attitude and a cheerful spirit. We should not dishonor God by grumbling, ungratefulness, negativity, or by bringing a dark cloud into the room. If we praise we will see a difference in our day. Things will go more smoothly.

2. ***Through Christ, live up to all the light you have.—Philippians 4:9***

a. "Wherever His word is obeyed with a sincere heart, there Christ abides."[112]

b. "Religion is not merely an emotion, a feeling. It is a principle which is interwoven with all the daily duties and transactions of life."[113]

c. Jesus desires that we bring our problems to Him and leave them at the cross.

d. If we would seek God and be converted everyday and by our own choice be joyous in God; if we would willingly obey and serve; we would find that we are no longer murmuring or complaining and that our difficulties and perplexing problems would be quickly solved.

3. **Recognize that there will be danger and losses**.

Read **Roman 8:28** and paraphrase it here: _____

_____

Read **John 17:15** and paraphrase it here: _____

_____

a. Jesus does not take us out of this world of sin and evil, dangers and trials. He promises to be our refuge. This was also Jesus' prayer for His disciples. (John 17)

b. We are not left alone to do His work or to be defenseless in the challenges that present themselves. We are to surrender our lives to His service, trusting that "we can never be placed in any position for which God has not made provision."[114]

c. "Those who exercise but little faith now, are in the greatest danger of falling under the power of satanic delusions and the decree to compel the conscience. And even if they endure the test they will be plunged into deeper distress and anguish in the time of trouble, because they have never made it a habit to trust in God. The lessons of faith which they have neglected they will be forced to learn under a terrible pressure of discouragement.

d. We should now acquaint ourselves with God by proving His promises."[115]

e. There are healing promises for every emergency and every trial. We are to seek the Lord during these times and plead with Him to show us a way out and show us the remedy to apply to our case as recorded in His word. If we do this, the enemy will find no place to lead us into unbelief. We will instead be filled with courage and faith in our Lord and Savior.

Assignment

1. Put these conditions into practice this week and claim Philippians 4:7 for **Peace of Mind**.

2. Read Romans 1:21 and notice that frustration is promised those who are not thankful! So let us be grateful!

3. Apply the following 10-point plan for rejoicing each day for the next ten days. This will help you live a life of rejoicing.

   a. Tomorrow morning, make a list of ten things for which you are thankful. During the day go over the list and praise the Lord for each blessing listed.

   b. Add ten more things for which you are thankful to your list each day for the next ten days. See how God will change your mental attitude. It is because of our ungratefulness, God says, that many of us are mentally frustrated. (See further Deuteronomy 28:15-68, especially verse 47).

4. This will help you to learn to rejoice at all times. Read Psalm 103:1-3, Psalm 34:1, and Nehemiah 8:10 and make promise cards or mark your *Bible*.

5. Read *Rejoicing in the Lord* on the following pages, and record your reflections.

Rejoicing in the Lord

The children of God are called upon to represent Christ and to show the goodness and mercy of the Lord. As Jesus has shown us the true character of the Father, so we are to show Christ to a world that does not know His kind love. Jesus prayed to His Father, *I sent them into the world, just as you sent me into the world. I in them and you in me, ... in order that the world may know that you sent me.*—John 17:18, 23 GNB.

The apostle Paul wrote to the disciples of Jesus, *You yourselves are the letter we have, ... for everyone to know and read.*—2 Corinthians 3:2. All Christ's children are like letters to the world. If we are Christ's followers, He sends us as a letter to our family. He sends us to the village and to the street where we live.

Jesus, living in us, wants to speak to the hearts of those who do not know Him. Perhaps they do not read the *Bible* or hear the voice that speaks to them in its pages. They do not see the love of God through His works. But if we truly represent Jesus, people may be led through us to see Him. They may understand something of His goodness and be won to love and serve Him.

Christians are light bearers along the way to heaven. They are to give to the world the light that shines upon them from Christ. Their lives and characters will show others what Christ is like and what it means to serve Him.

When we represent Christ, we show to others that it is a pleasure to work for Him. Christians know that this is really true. Christians who complain and are unhappy give others a wrong idea of God and the Christian life. They make people think that God is not pleased to have His children happy. This is too bad, for they are telling something about their heavenly Father that is not true.

Satan is pleased when he can lead the children of God into doubt and unhappiness. He delights to see us mistrust God. He wants us to doubt God's willingness and power to save us. He loves to have us feel that God will lead us into harm.

Satan wants us to feel that the Lord does not have pity for us. But he is not telling the truth. He fills our minds with false ideas about God. He tries to make us think about these wrong ideas instead of God's goodness. He wants us to distrust God and complain about the way He leads us.

Satan tries to make the Christian life seem dark and unhappy. He wants it to appear hard and unpleasant; and some Christians may, by the way they act, make people think that serving God is hard. This makes it seem that they agree with Satan.

Many people, walking along the path of life, think and talk about their mistakes. They talk about how they have failed, and their hearts are filled with sorrow. A woman who had been doing this wrote to me while I was in Europe. She was very unhappy and asked me for some words of hope. The night after I read her letter I dreamed I was in a garden. The one who seemed to be the owner of the garden was leading me along its paths.

I was gathering the flowers and enjoying their sweet smell. Then this woman, who had been walking by my side, called me to look at the ugly thorns that were in her way. There she was, sadly crying. She was not walking in the path or following the guide, but she was walking among the thorns.

"Oh," she cried, "what a pity that this beautiful garden is spoiled with thorns." Then the guide said, "Let the thorns alone, for they will only wound you. Gather the roses, the lilies, and the pinks."

We should think of the good times in our lives. Have we had precious hours when our hearts were filled with joy as the Spirit of God spoke to us? When we look back over our lives, do we see many pleasant times? Are God's promises like the sweet flowers growing beside our path? Can we let their beauty and sweetness fill our hearts with joy?

Thorns will only wound us and make us sad. If we gather thorns and give them to other people, we are turning from God's goodness. We are keeping people around us from walking in the path of life.

We should not try to remember all the unpleasant things that have happened to us in the past. We should not talk of our sins and sorrow over them. We would soon be overcome and feel that we had no hope. A person without hope sees only darkness. He is shutting out the light of God from himself, and throwing a shadow across the path of others.

Growing in the "YES" of God

We may thank God for the bright pictures He presents to us. Let us bring together God's wonderful promises so that we may look at them often. The Son of God left His Father's throne and covered His divine nature with human flesh. He became a man so that He could save people from the power of Satan. He won the battle with evil for us and opened heaven to show us its glory.

Let us study how people are lifted from the pit of sin. Let us learn how they are again brought close to God. Picture in your mind how we, through faith in our Redeemer, are clothed with Christ's righteousness. We are lifted by faith to His throne. God wants us to think about all these things.

We do not honor God and we sadden His Holy Spirit when we seem to doubt God's love and His promises. How would a mother feel if her children were always talking against her? How would she feel if they acted as though she wanted them to suffer? Her whole life's work has been to bring comfort to them. It would break her heart if they doubted her love. How would parents feel if they were treated in this way by their children?

What can our heavenly Father think of us if we do not trust His love? This love has led Him to give His own Son that we might have life. The apostle wrote, *He gave us his Son—will he not also freely give us all things?*—Romans 8:32. And yet how many people by their acts, if not by their words, turn from His love. They say, "The Lord does not mean this for me. Perhaps He loves others, but He does not love me."

These thoughts are harmful, for every word of doubt invites Satan to tempt us. Our own doubts are strengthened, and we turn the holy angels away from us. We should not speak a word of doubt when Satan tempts us. If we choose to open the door to him, our minds will be filled with doubts and questions. Speaking in a doubting way is not only bad for us, but it plants a seed that will grow and bear fruit in the lives of others. It may be impossible to stop the influence of our words.

We ourselves may be able to turn away from the time of doubting and from Satan's leading. But others who have heard and believed us may not be able to forget our words. How important it is that we speak only those things that will give spiritual strength and life!

Angels are listening to hear what kind of report we are giving to the world about our heavenly Master. Let our thoughts and words be of Him who stands before His Father. When we take the hand of a friend, let praise to God be on our lips and in our hearts. This will turn our friend's thoughts to Jesus.

Everyone has trials, sorrows, and temptations. We must not tell our troubles to people, but take everything to God in prayer. We should make it a rule never to speak a word of doubt. We can do much to brighten the lives of others. Our words of hope and holy cheer will make them stronger.

Satan is tempting many brave people to do wrong. They are almost ready to faint in the battle with self and the powers of evil. We should not make it harder for such people. We may cheer them with brave, hopeful words that will help them along the way. Thus Christ's light shines from us. *We do not live for ourselves only.*—Romans 14:7 GNB. We may be helping others by our words and acts without knowing it. Or we may be causing people to lose hope and to turn away from Christ and the truth.

Many people have a wrong idea of the life and character of Christ. They do not think that He was friendly and happy. They think He was cold, severe, and without joy. They let this idea of Christ darken their lives.

It is often said that Jesus shed tears but never smiled. Our Savior was indeed a Man of sorrows. He knew what sadness was, for He opened His heart to all the sorrows of the people. His life was shadowed with pain and cares, but His spirit was never broken. His face wore a look of peace and joy. Happiness flowed from His heart. Wherever He went He brought rest and peace, joy and gladness.

Our Savior was deeply thoughtful but never gloomy. The lives of those who follow Him will be like His. Christ's followers know they have a great work to do for Him. They will not be foolish, rough, and loud. They will not repeat coarse jokes. The faith of Jesus will give them a peace that will flow like a river. His peace will make the light of joy shine. It will bring true happiness, cheer, and smiles. Christ did not come to be waited on. He came to help people. When His love is in our heart, we will follow His example.

If we keep thinking of the unkind and unfair acts of other people, we will not be able to love them as Christ loves us. But if we think of Christ's wonderful love and pity for us, this same spirit will flow out to others. We should love and respect one another even though we cannot help seeing their faults. We should be humble and not trust ourselves. If we are patient with the faults of others, we will become less selfish, and more kind-hearted and generous.

David wrote, *Trust in the Lord and do good; live in the land and be safe.*— Psalm 37:3 GNB.

"Trust in the Lord." Each day has its cares and problems. When we meet our friends we are ready to talk about our troubles. We talk and worry because we are afraid hard times will come. A person might think that we had no pitying, loving Savior waiting to hear our prayers. We do not speak as if He is ready to help us in every time of need.

Some people are always afraid and expecting trouble. Every day God's love is around them, but they do not see His blessings. Their minds are filled with fear of something unpleasant which might come, or they worry about some real, small problem that they have. Worry keeps them from seeing many things for which they could be thankful. Problems should make them turn to God, who is their Helper. Instead, they allow hard experiences to separate them from Him.

Should we doubt God? Should we distrust Him? Jesus is our friend. All heaven is interested in what happens to us. We should not let our daily worries make us afraid. If we do, we shall always have something to make us unhappy. Worry does not help us bear our trials.

We may be worried about our business. The future looks darker and darker. We are afraid we shall lose what we have. But we must not give up hope. We may lay all our cares upon God. We may ask Him to show us how to care for our business so that we will not suffer loss. Then we must do all we can to bring about the best results. Jesus has promised His help, but He expects us to do what we can. When we have done all we can with God's help, we may accept the results cheerfully.

God does not want His people to be weighed down with care. But our Lord does not try to mislead us. He does not say to us, "Do not fear; there are no dangers in your path." He knows there are problems and dangers, and He tells us so. He does not say He will take His people out of this world of sin and evil, but He points us to a never-failing place of safety.

Jesus' prayer for His disciples was *I do not ask you to take them out of the world, but I do ask you to keep them safe from the Evil One.*—John 17:15

164

GNB. Jesus said, *The world will make you suffer. But be brave! I have defeated the world.*—John 16:33 GNB.

In His sermon on the mount, Christ taught His disciples precious lessons about their need to trust in God. These lessons were also to help all of God's children. They have come down to our time to bring us help and comfort.

The Savior spoke of the birds of the air. He said that the birds sing their songs of praise without worrying about their needs. *They do not plant seeds, gather a harvest and put it in barns; yet your Father in heaven takes care of them."* The Savior asked, *Aren't you worth much more than birds?*—Matthew 6:26 GNB.

The great Father opens His hands and gives enough for the needs of all His creatures. The birds of the air are always in His thoughts. He does not drop food into their bills, but He provides for all their needs. They must gather the grain He has scattered for them. They must find what they need to build their nests and feed their young.

The birds sing as they hunt for their food. They sing because our "Father in heaven takes care of them." Are not we who are able to worship God of more value than the birds of the air? Will not our Creator, the One who keeps us alive, also care for us? He who made us will give us everything we need if we trust Him.

Christ spoke of the flowers of the field. The heavenly Father made the beautiful flowers to show His love for His earthly children. Christ said, "Look how the wild flowers grow!" The simple beauty of these wildflowers was more attractive than the splendid robes of King Solomon. The most beautiful clothes that people can make cannot compare with the grace and shining beauty of the flowers of God's creation.

Jesus said, *It is God who clothes the wild grass—grass that is here today and gone tomorrow, burned up in the oven. Won't he be all the more sure to clothe you? What little faith you have!*—Matthew 6:30 GNB.

God, the divine Artist, gives the simple flowers their many colors. Some of these flowers live for only a day, yet He makes them beautiful and perfect. How much greater care will He have for people He has created in His own likeness! Christ gave us this lesson to teach us not to worry. We are not to doubt or lose our faith.

Growing in the "YES" of God

The Lord wants all His sons and daughters to be happy and to have peace. He wants them to trust and obey. Jesus said, *Peace is what I leave with you; it is my own peace that I give you. I do not give it as the world does. Do not be worried and upset; do not be afraid. I have told you this so that my joy may be in you and that your joy may be complete.*—John 14:27; 15:11 GNB.

Happiness that is gotten from being selfish soon passes away. This happiness leaves a person lonely and filled with sorrow. But there is real, lasting joy in the service of God. Christians have a Guide to lead them. They need not be sad over things they have done. They may miss some pleasures in this world, but they can be happy as they think of the joys they will have in heaven.

Even in this world Christians have the joy of knowing they can walk and talk with Christ. They may have the light of His love and the comfort of knowing that He is with them. Every step in life may bring them closer to Jesus and make them know more of His love. Every step may bring them nearer to the blessed home of peace.

Then let us hold to our faith in God. Let us have a hope that is stronger than ever. *The Lord has helped us all the way*—1 Samuel 7:12 GNB, and He will help us to the end.

Let us remember what the Lord has done to comfort us and to save us from Satan, our enemy. Let us keep fresh in our minds all the tender mercies God has shown us. Think of the tears He has wiped away, and the pain He has helped us bear. He has taken away our fears and worries, and has given us everything we need. These blessings from God should make us strong to bear the trials during the rest of our life journey.

We cannot help thinking about the trials and tests we will face before the end of the world. But we can look back as well as forward and say, "The Lord has helped us all the way." *And as your days, so shall your strength be.*—Deuteronomy 33:25 RSV. The trials will not be greater than the strength God will give us. So let us take up our work where we find it, believing we will be strong enough to meet whatever comes.

Someday the gates of heaven will be thrown open to welcome God's children. From the lips of the King of glory will fall a blessing like rich music: *Come, you that are blessed by my Father! Come and possess the kingdom*

166

which has been prepared for you ever since the creation of the world.— Matthew 25:34 GNB.

The redeemed will be welcomed to the home that Jesus is preparing for them. In heaven there will be no wicked people. The friends of the redeemed will be people who have overcome Satan through divine grace and have formed perfect characters. Every desire to sin will have been taken away by the blood of Christ. The redeemed will shine with Christ's glory, which is much brighter than the sun. And what is more, the beauty of His character will also shine out through them. They will stand without fault before God and will have the same blessings as the angels.

A beautiful heavenly home is ready for the redeemed. *Will you gain anything if you win the whole world but lose your life?—*Matthew 16:26 GNB. A person may be poor now, but in the gift of eternal life he owns greater wealth than the world can ever give. A person redeemed by Jesus, made clean from all sin, and serving God is of more value than the whole world. There is joy in heaven before God over every person that is redeemed. This joy makes the heavenly angels sing holy songs of victory.[116]

"Prayer is in every deed the pulse of spiritual life ... Perseverance and believing prayer means a strong and abundant life."
—Andrew Murray,
Let Prayer Change Your life
(Tirabassi), p. 42

Record of Experiences

Record of Experiences

This record of experiences will help you keep a list of the problems you had, the promises you claimed and the date your prayers were answered. It will help to increase your faith in the future when you can look back and see how God so miraculously intervened.

Date Asked	Problem	Promise Text	Date Answered	How Answered

Speak Lord, Your servant is listening—1 Samuel 3:9-10 NIV

Weekly Reflections

_____

_____

_____

_____

_____

_____

_____

_____

_____

_____

_____

_____

"God stands back of every promise that He has made and the honor of His throne is staked for fulfillment of His word to us."

—Praying in the "YES" of God, p. 88

Lesson Ten—The Relationship of Faith and Prayer

Let us therefore come boldly to the throne of grace that we may obtain mercy and find grace to help in time of need.
—Hebrews 4:16

*(Please refer to pages 86-89 in **Living Volume One: Praying in the "YES" of God** while you are studying this chapter.)*

Introduction

What we have studied so far:

1. The **Prayer of Reception**
2. The Conditions to answered prayer and how to fulfill them.
3. How to turn Problems into Opportunities.
4. How to avoid presumption.
5. Devotional and study ideas.

6. The **Prayer of Commitment**

   Basic principles regarding sickness and health.

7. The Holy Spirit

   a. The meaning of happiness.

   b. Our role as channels of the Holy Spirit.

   c. A brief overview of Intercessory Prayer.

   d. The difference between hospitality and entertaining.

8. The science and challenge of Christian witnessing and soul-winning.

9. The study of the spiritual principles involved in receiving and maintaining **Peace of Mind**.

In this lesson we will look at factors that weaken and strengthen our faith.

"The practice of telling our difficulties to others only makes us weak, and brings no strength to them. It lays upon them the burden of our spiritual infirmities, which they cannot relieve. We seek the strength of erring, finite man, when we might have the strength of the unerring, infinite God …

It is not the capabilities you now possess or ever will have that will give you success. It is that which the Lord can do for you … The Lord is rich in resources; He owns the world. Look heavenward in faith."[117] He has invited us *to come boldly before His throne of grace.*—Hebrews 4:16

Problems Reveal Opportunities

+ Opportunities for inner reflection and purification

+ Opportunities for adventures with the Savior

+ Opportunities for trust and relationship to grow with God as you wait and watch for solutions.

+ Opportunities to experience God active in your life.

Problems

Reveal

Opportunities!

Better

Let

Emmanuel

Mediate

Solutions.

Factors That Weaken and Strengthen Faith.

Factors that will contribute to the weakening of faith

1. **Cherishing secret sin.**

   Read **Psalm 66:18** and paraphrase it here: _____

   _____

   Read **James 4:17** and paraphrase it here: _____

   _____

   Read **Proverbs 28:9** and paraphrase it here: _____

   _____

   Read **Isaiah 59:2** and paraphrase it here: _____

   _____

2. **Studying the *Bible* without prayer**.

   a. Before opening the pages of the *Bible*, we must ask the Holy Spirit to be our Teacher.

b. Never should the *Bible* be studied without prayer. The archenemy, Satan, would desire to take advantage of us, and conduct the *Bible* study to lead us into falsehood.

c. If God's Word were consistently studied, by the Holy Spirit's guidance, and the promises of God claimed as He has instructed, men would have an understanding of mind, a character without question, and a well-grounded, stable purpose, missing from the multitude of today' society.

3. **Being spasmodic and neglectful in our prayer life**

a. *...in everything by prayer ...*—Philippians 4:6

b. If we neglect prayer, or pray only occasionally or as convenient, we will lose our hold on God.

c. Great men of the *Bible* had constant and consistent prayer lives.

Read **Genesis 5:24** and paraphrase it here: _____

_____

Read **Genesis 6:9** and paraphrase it here: _____

_____

Read **Daniel 6:10** and paraphrase it here: _____

_____

4. **Telling our troubles to others.**

a. *It is better to take refuge in the Lord than to put confidence in man.*—Psalm 118:8

b. Have no anxiety about anything but in everything by prayer and supplication with thanksgiving let your requests be made known to God.—Philippians 4:6

c. We should take all our problems to God. Bring Him all our cares and perplexities. Come to Him as your confidante. Trust all to God.

d. 'The more you talk faith, the more faith you will have. The more you dwell upon discouragement, talking to others about your trials and enlarging upon then, to enlist the sympathy which you crave, the more discouragement and trials you will have."[118]

e. If someone comes to us with their problems, listen to them and lead them to Christ, the Wonderful Counselor.

f. For further study, see: Jeremiah 17:5-8, and Micah 7:5-7.

> **Reflection Thoughts**—Read and study the scriptures listed above. What do the verses listed here mean to you? Journal your thoughts.

---

5. **Allowing distrust to come in.**

Read and reflect on **Numbers 14**—The story of the children of Israel and the spies of the promised land.

Factors that will contribute to the strengthening of faith.

1. **Studying the Word of God and praying for the enlightenment of the Holy Spirit.**

   Read **Romans 10:17** and paraphrase it here: _____

   _____

   Read **John 16:13** and paraphrase it here: _____

   _____

   Our faith must be exercised by diligent, persevering study of the Word.

2. **Claiming promises for little things in which we need help as well as for larger problems.**

Growing in the "YES" of God

Read **1 Peter 5:7** and paraphrase it here: _____

_____

God wants us to share our small perplexities as well as our largest problems, because He is mindful of all that concerns us.

3. **Talking and acting as if our faith were invincible.**

   Read **Proverbs 18:21** and paraphrase it here: _____

   _____

   a. Read and reflect on the story of David and Goliath in 1 Samuel 17:45-50.

   b. "Never allow yourself to talk in a hopeless, discouraged way. If you do you will lose much. By looking at appearances and complaining when difficulties and pressures come, you give evidence of a sickly, enfeebled faith. Talk and act as if your faith was invincible."[119]

   c. "If you want faith, talk faith; talk hopefully, cheerfully."[120]

   d. "It is a law of nature that our thoughts and feelings are encouraged and strengthened as we give them utterance."[121]

4. **Speaking encouraging words.**

   ...say to those who are of a fearful heart, Be strong, fear not!—Isaiah 35:3-10

5. **Speaking of our daily blessings and answers to prayer.**

   a. *...Every day I will bless thee, and praise Thy name ...*—Psalm 145:1-21 KJV

   b. Praise dispels the enemy. God inhabits the praises of His people.

6. **Work for the salvation of others**

   a. *... and he who waters will himself be watered* [reaping the generosity he has sown].—Proverbs 11:25 AMPC. *The fruit of the [uncompromisingly] righteous is a tree of life, and he who is wise captures human lives [for God, as a fisher of men—he gathers and receives them for eternity].*—Proverbs 11:30 AMPC.

176

b.   "If you will go to work as Christ designs that His disciples shall, and win souls for Him, you will feel the need of a deeper experience and a greater knowledge in divine things, and will hunger and thirst after righteousness. You will plead with God, and your faith will be strengthened, and your soul will drink deeper drafts at the well of salvation. Encountering opposition and trials will drive you to the *Bible* and prayer. You will grow in grace and the knowledge of Christ, and will develop a rich experience."[122]

"One of the divine plans for growth is impartation. The Christian is to gain strength by strengthening others. He that watereth shall be watered also himself. This is not merely a promise; it is a divine law."[123]

Promises are the secret to the building of Christian character. "If with a humble heart you seek divine guidance in every trouble and perplexity, His word is pledged that a gracious answer will be given you"[124] "So with all the promises of God's word. In them He is speaking as directly as if we could listen to His voice. It is in these promises that Christ communicates to us His grace and power. They are leaves from the tree which is *for the healing of the nations.—* Revelations 22:2. Received, assimilated, they are to be the strength of the character, the inspiration and sustenance of the life, nothing else can have such healing power. Nothing besides can impart the courage and faith which give vital energy to the whole being."[125]

Promises of God should be committed to memory. "Make the promises of God your own. Then when test and trial come, these promises will be to you glad springs of heavenly comfort. Temptations often appear irresistible because, through neglect of prayer and the study of the *Bible* the tempted one cannot readily remember God's promises and meet Satan with the scripture weapons ...The heart that is stored with the precious truths of God's word is fortified against the temptation of Satan, against impure thoughts and unholy actions. Let us commit its precious promises to memory, so that, when we are deprived of our *Bibles*, we may still be in possession of the Word of God."[126]

"The teachings of Christ must previously have been stored in the mind in order for the spirit of God to bring them to our remembrance in the time of peril. *Thy word have I hid in mine heart,* said David, *that I might not sin against Thee.—*Psalm 119:11 KJV[127]

Conclusion to this Course

A special reason for learning this material is that by getting acquainted with God through proving His **promises** in Jesus Christ we prepare for the time of trouble. We see the strength that has been won for us on the cross of Christ.

"Those who exercise but little **faith** now, are in the greatest danger of falling under the power of satanic delusions and the decree to compel the conscience. And even if they endure the test they will be plunged into deeper distress and anguish in the time of trouble, because they have never made it a habit to trust in God. The lessons of **faith** which they have neglected they will be forced to learn under a terrible pressure of discouragement. We should now acquaint ourselves with God by proving His **promises**."[128]

DISCLAIMER

Those who know me are aware I have a home full of books and many, many file cabinets full of material. Some of this information I have filed and categorized since I was a very young child. As I became a teenager, if I saw an article or quotation I liked, I wrote it down as well. Sometimes, I just wrote down my own thoughts and filed them or put them on a 3 x 5 card and stuck them away. As I continued to grow and learn, I found when you keep material you need to record the sources as well. I hadn't done that with all the saved material.

I have many compilations of material I put together when I started speaking many years ago. I do not know for sure if all the references were cited there either. Some of these compilations I have used in this book.

To the best of my knowledge I have not included anyone else's work in my book unless I have given the reference or had permission to use it. If anything got past me, I humbly ask your forgiveness. My intention is to bring people to a deeper love and knowledge of our Savior, certainly not to claim someone else's work as my own. I hope this apology is for naught, but since I am such a hoarder of information, I felt it appropriate to waylay a potential problem by any oversight

I would also like to share my heart regarding the quotations I used in this book. Because I have quoted a particular author does not mean I endorse all they teach or believe. If they have made a profound statement that punctuates what I am teaching, then I have quoted them and credited their work. I like to look for the "good" in everyone and accentuate the positive.

"The Lord desires to position us for eternal glory and blessing that last forever. But the degree to which we will enjoy future rewards with Him rests upon our ability to delay gratification now. Can we say no to the things of this world grabbing our affections, our attention, and our very life?"
—Rabbi Schneider,
The Book of Revelation Decoded,
p. 167

Appendix A

Resources

Please feel free to copy the following pages as you need them. You will also find printable versions on our website:

FreedomInSurrender.net/Resources

Daily Prayer Sheet

For Forgiveness

Dear Heavenly Father,

I **ask** that You will forgive me for _____;

I **believe** that You have forgiven me because You have promised in 1 John 1:9;

I **thank** You that You have forgiven me.

In Jesus' name, Amen.

For Intercession and Soul Winning

Dear Heavenly Father,

I **ask** that You will give me life to give _____;

I **believe** that You are giving me life to give him/her because You have promised in 1 John 5:16;

I **thank** You that You have given me life to give him/her.

In Jesus' name, Amen.

For the Holy Spirit

Dear Heavenly Father,

I **ask** that You will give me the Holy Spirit;

I **believe** that You are giving me the Holy Spirit because You have promised in Luke 11:13;

I **thank** You that You have given me the Holy Spirit.

In Jesus' name, Amen.

"Combining fasting with prayer can result in a spiritual atomic bomb that pulls down spiritual strongholds and releases the power of God in your life and the life of ..."
—Bill Bright,

Bible *Promises*

By getting acquainted with God through proving His promises in Jesus, we come to know God as our personal Friend and Savior. We learn the victory and hope won for us on the cross of Christ.

PROMISES FOR FORGIVENESS

Isaiah 43:25	He will not remember our sins
Jeremiah 31:34	Forgive iniquity and remember sin no more
Romans 8:1	No condemnation
1 John 1:9	If we confess, He will forgive

PROMISES FOR CHRIST CHARACTER AND SPIRITUAL ISSUES

Deuteronomy 5:32-33	Walk in way—do what Lord has commanded, so you may live, Prosper and prolong your days in the land you possess
Joshua 1:3, 9	Give you everywhere you put foot and be strong, courageous; do not be terrified or discouraged
Psalm 20:6	Saves His anointed. Answers with saving power.
Jeremiah 31:33	Write Law in our hearts
Jeremiah 32:27	God of all flesh can do anything
Jeremiah 32:38	You shall be My people
Ezekiel 36:26	A new heart and spirit
Luke 11:13	The infilling of the Holy Spirit
Luke 12:12	Holy Spirit teaches us what to say

Growing in the "YES" of God

Luke 24:45	Understand scripture
John 1:12	Receive Jesus, become sons of God
John 14:26	Holy Spirit teach & bring to our remembrance
John 16:13	Spirit of truth will guide you to truth
Galatians 5:22-26	Fruit of Spirit
Ephesians 3:16	Inner man strengthened by Spirit
Ephesians 4:24	Put on new man
Philippians 2:5	Mind of Jesus
Colossians 3:15	Peace of God
1 Thessalonians 2:13	Words of truth will work in us
1 Thessalonians 3:13	Establish our heat in holiness
1 Thessalonians 5:24	He will help us do what He has called us to do
Hebrews 3:14	Partakers of Christ
Hebrews 10:19-22	Come boldly to throne of grace
2 Peter 1:4	Divine nature

PROMISES FOR WITNESSING

Exodus 4:12	Teach us what to say
Job 33:3	Utter knowledge clearly
Isaiah 50:4	Have tongue of the learned, know what to speak
Isaiah 65:23	Labor not in vain
Jeremiah 1:7	He will send us

Jeremiah 1:9	God will put His words in our mouth

PROMISES ESPECIALLY FOR FAMILY

Genesis 2:18	Companion suited to our needs
Genesis 3:15	Enmity between our children and evil associates
Genesis 3:16	Desire to husband
Genesis 16:11	Lord heard misery and gave son
Genesis 17:20	As for Ishmael, I have heard thee, I will bless him—fruitful
Genesis 29:34	Leah not loved, God heard—gave son
Psalm 86:16	Save sons
Proverbs 1:8	Sons hear instruction
Proverbs 3:1	Sons forget not law
Isaiah 49:25	God will save our children
Hosea 2:19-20	Betrothed forever to spouse and God, in righteousness, loving-kindness, faithfulness
Zephaniah 3:13	Not do iniquity, nor speak lies
Malachi 2:5	Have Godly children from union
Mark 10:8-9	The two become one
Luke 1:17	Turn heats of fathers to children
Luke 2:40	Child grow in spirit, wisdom, and grace
John 17:21	Be one in Jesus
1 Corinthians 11:3	Head of man is Christ, head of woman is man

Growing in the "YES" of God

Ephesians 5:22	Wives submit to husbands
Ephesians 5:25	Husbands love wives
Ephesians 6:1	Children obey
Ephesians 6:4	Parents don't provoke children
Philippians 2:2-4	Likeminded, same love
Hebrews 13:1	Brotherly love
Hebrews 13:4	Marriage bed undefiled

PROMISES TO SAVE FROM THE DEVIL AND TEMPTATIONS

Exodus 44:23	Know difference between holy & profane
2 Kings 13:4	Lord listened to him for He saw how severely His people were being oppressed
Psalm 17:6-7	Those who take refuge in Him, He will save
Isaiah 33:15-16	Walk righteously and speak right, no contemplating evil, reject gain from extortion, any bribes or murder
Isaiah 54:17	No weapon formed against us will prosper
Luke 4:8	Satan behind us, worship Lord
John 8:36	Jesus will set you free from whatever binds you
John 10:27-28	Will not be taken from Jesus' hand
Acts 26:18	Turn from power of Satan
Romans 16:20	God of peace will bruise Satan
1 Corinthians 10:13	No temptation more than we are able to bear

2 Corinthians 7:1	Cleansing from filthiness of flesh and spirit
2 Corinthians 10:3-6	Casting down imaginations and everything that exalteth against the knowledge of God
Ephesians 6:11-19	Armor of God
Colossians 2:5	Triumph over Satan
James 4:7	Resist devil, he will flee

PROMISES OF JOY AND ASSURANCE

Nehemiah 3:10	Joy of the Lord our strength
John 14:13	I will not leave you comfortless
Romans 8:28	All things work together for good
John 15:11	My joy be in you
Psalm 34:3	Happy is man who takes refuge in Lord
Psalm 16:11	Show path of life fullness of joy
Psalm 32:1	Happy whose disobedience forgiven
Galatians 5:22-23	Fruits of the Spirit
Proverbs 3:5-6	Trust in Lord, make straight paths
Job 22:21	Acquaint self with Him and be at peace
Joshua 1:9	Be strong and of good courage
Luke 21:36	Pray for strength to escape
3 John 2	Enjoy good health
1 John 5:5	Overcome world through Jesus
Psalm 34:18	Lord close to brokenhearted

Growing in the "YES" of God

Jeremiah 29:11	Lord had good plans
Psalm 32:8	Make you wise; guide you and watch over
Isaiah 26:3	Perfect Peace

GENERAL PROMISES

Exodus 3:13	Fill with wisdom, knowledge, understanding
Exodus 5:13	Fulfill work, daily tasks
Deuteronomy 1:21	Fear not nor be discouraged
1 Kings 9:3	I have heard prayer and plea, I have consecrated temple which you built by putting My name there forever
Nehemiah 8:10	Joy of Lord is our strength
Psalm 19:3	Hears every speech and language
Psalm 19:13	Keep from presumptuous sins
Psalm 19:14	Words of mouth and meditation of heart acceptable
Psalm 28:8	Lord is our strength
Psalm 31:24	Courage
Psalm 32:8	God will instruct, teach and guide
Psalm 34:7	Angels will encamp round about
Psalm 34:13	Keep tongue from evil
Psalm 46:1	God is refuge and strength
Psalm 56:11	Trust in God not man
Psalm 73:28	Put trust in God

Psalm 86:11	Learn God's ways
Psalm 103:3	Heal our diseases
Psalm 119:105	Word is our lamp
Psalm 138:8	Lord will perfect that which concerns us
Psalm 141:3	Set a watch, Lord, over our mouth
Isaiah 40:31	Strength renewed
Isaiah 41:17-18	Poor and needy search for water—I will answer them
Isaiah 49:8	In an acceptable time have I heard you, day of salvation, I have helped you
Isaiah 65:24	God will answer even before we call
Hosea 14:4	Heal backsliding
Jeremiah 33:3	Reveal secrets
Malachi 3:10	Windows of heaven opened
Matthew 9:29	According to our faith
Mark 5:34	Faith makes us whole
Luke 12:2	Reveal secrets
John 11:22	Ask and it will be given
Romans 8:28	All things work together for good
Romans 12:13	Given to hospitality
Romans 15:4	Scriptures for learning and hope
1 Corinthians 3:9	Laborers with God

Growing in the "YES" of God

2 Corinthians 4:16	Inward man renewed
Galatians 1:10	Not men pleasers but servants of God
Ephesians 4:29	No corrupt communication
Ephesians 4:32	Kind, tenderhearted
Philippians 3:18-21	Appetite
Colossians 1:9-14	Filled with knowledge of God's will
2 Timothy 1:7	Not fear but love
Hebrews 12:150	No bitterness
James 1:5	Wisdom
James 5:15	Prayer of faith shall save sick
1 Peter 2:11	Abstain from fleshly lusts
1 Peter 3:8	Be of one mind, compassion
1 Peter 5:6	Humble self, God will exalt
1 Peter 5:7	Cast cares upon God
1 John 3:18	Love in deed and truth
1 John 4:18	No fear
Revelation 3:8	Keep word, open door to God
Revelation 3:18	Anoint eyes that we may see

Record of Experiences

Record of Experiences

This record of experiences will help you keep a list of the problems you had, the promises you claimed and the date your prayers were answered. It will help to increase your faith in the future when you can look back and see how God so miraculously intervened.

Date Asked	Problem	Promise Text	Date Answered	How Answered

Speak Lord, Your servant is listening—1 Samuel 3:9-10 NIV

Weekly Reflections

_____

_____

_____

_____

_____

_____

_____

_____

_____

_____

_____

_____

_____

Mid Study Review

1. We have been studying the Prayer of Faith , also   known   as   the
   Prayer of Reception or Petition .

2. **The three Vocal Conditions to claiming *Bible* Promises are:**

   ✦ ASK—Matthew 7:7

   ✦ BELIEVE—Mark 11:24

   ✦ THANK—Colossians 4:2

   extra points if you can remember the text for each!

3. **Name the 15 General Conditions in claiming *Bible* Promises.**

Need of God	Ask In Jesus Name
Perseverance	Diligence
Seek First Kingdom	Patience
Faith	Love
Forgiveness	Concern For Others
Obedience	Pure Heart

   Responsive Heart/Humility/Repentance

4. **There are approximately (circle one) Promises or clusters of Promises in the *Bible*.**

   a. ~~1000~~   b. ~~3000~~   c. ~~5000~~   d. **7000**

5. **Name two objectives of this class: To emphasize the great need of God's people for effective prayer life.**

   Any of the following points

   + To prove that God stands behind His word and He can be trusted.

   + To confirm that miracles are not outdated.

   + To recognize Christ as our personal Friend and Savior and realize His interest in each detail of our lives.

   + To demonstrate the reality of the Prayer of Faith, especially the Prayer of Reception, by active experimentation.

   + To help develop a deeper relationship with God through application of the conditions to answered prayer and an understanding of the divine science of prayer.

   + To recognize that adventure with Jesus equals peace of mind.

   + To understand how problems can reveal opportunities.

   + To simplify witnessing/making disciples to a way of life.

6. **Name two ways to guard against presumption when claiming God's Promises.**

   a. Do not leave any conditions unfulfilled

   b. Do not claim that prayer will always be answered in the very way for the particular thing desired.

APPENDIX B

Leaders and Teachers Guide

"It is only life that can beget life. He alone has life who is connected with the Source of life; and only such can be a channel of life. In order that the teacher may accomplish the object of his work, he should be a living embodiment of truth, a living channel through which wisdom and life may flow. A pure life, the result of sound principles and right habits, should therefore be regarded as his most essential qualifications."[129]

Growing in the "YES" of God-Instructions for Leaders

This course, in its previous form, was originally introduced in 1970. It has years of tried and true instruction, participation, application, and proven success behind it. We have found the most effective and longest-lasting results come when the Lead Pastor and leaders have been through the class before it is presented to the church at large. If your congregants go through the class without the pastors' endorsement they may be like seeds planted among thorns, soon to be choked out. Once the pastor has been through the class, has an understanding of the material being taught, and has made personal application, you can expect more encouragement, interest, and excitement in support of your endeavors to teach others. You should work towards training spiritual leaders to run the program so that its success is not dependent upon the pastor's availability to run it.

Many have the theological understanding of the *Bible* but it's a personal relationship that is lacking. Often God's promises are spoken of but they are not applied to life. With this course, our intention is to change lives and help people realize that Jesus knows them, loves them, and is concerned with every detail of their life. Use what you learn here as you would use tools in building a house—appropriately, efficiently and timely.

Prior to beginning class, you need to choose a time that will enable participants to be punctual. Allow an hour and a half for class. Consider your attendees and offer babysitting if necessary. Depending upon the time you are conducting class and the ages and number of children needing care, you may have to have two groups; one for those who can stay up and one for those who need to go to sleep.

Growing in the "YES" of God

Several weeks prior to class have a sign-up sheet in the foyer. Please advise your students to call if they are not going to be able to make class. We strongly recommend that no classes be skipped for any reasons. If any are, please make every effort to get them caught up during the week. Also, as a leader, it is critical to the success of the course that you check in with each student during the week. If possible make this a personal visit. Find out how they're doing and if they are doing their studies. Your interest and encouragement may make all the difference in their staying with the course to conclusion. Some may be dealing with pressing trials and are anxious to see God's intervention. Whether your visit is personal or by phone, be sure you pray for them before you leave. Pray for them daily.

Each class should be conducted with a similar format. In the first 20-30 minutes, begin with opening prayer, followed by a time of sharing. Sharing testimonies is as important as the lessons themselves. Students' testimonies are encouraging to the other students and reinforce what they have learned. The last hour is in teaching and discussing the lesson. Close by dividing into groups of three and have them each pray aloud, following the prayers claiming the promises for the Holy Spirit and for God to give them life to share with whomever they have chosen to intercede. During the class study time, you may have various leaders take certain sections for instruction, assuming you have co-leaders, or you may have your students take turns reading sections, stopping them when you need to interject or punctuate key points with explanation or stories.

Start with opening prayer

Our loving Father who art in heaven, we are so thankful for the opportunity to share with our church family and friends the marvelous miracles You have worked in our lives. We are thankful that You are such a loving and kind Father and for giving your children all the power, all the resources, and all the wisdom of the universe to perfect and transform our character. We want to be more like you.

We pray that you will send the Holy Spirit to be with us during our class. We believe that You are sending the Holy Spirit as you promise in Luke 11:13, and we thank You for sending the Holy Spirit.

Please dear Father, be with each student as he shares his experience, giving him words from heaven that will reach the hearts of each one listening. If there is even one person here today that is not living a life of spiritual victory, but is instead living in defeat, frustration, and anxiety; or if anyone here is uncertain of his eternal destiny, we pray that these experiences might be the motivating factor in leading that person to the full joy of complete salvation. We ask these things in the name of Jesus our Lord and Savior. Amen.

Introduction to read to class

Every member of our **Praying in the "YES" of God** class should become familiar with the text found in 2 Peter 1:4 and what it means. It is a text, the power, the meaning; the force of which we hope will become very real and very precious to each of you.

2 Peter 1:4 RSV says, *by which He has granted to us His precious and very great promises, that through these you may escape from the corruption that is in the world because of passion, and become partakers of the divine nature.*

Please notice the word "promises" because it is one of the keywords of this verse. "Divine nature" are the other two keywords. Here we have a precious promise in this text that tells us that you and I today do not have to lead lives of failure. We do not have to lead lives of defeat or frustration. This text tells us that we may become partakers of the divine nature of God in our heart and in our life. This text not only tells us what we can have, but how we can have it.

According to our *Bible*, the way we can become partakers of the divine nature is through the promises of God's word. There are over 7000 of them. Anyone can learn to know which promise is applicable, then claim it, and appropriate it in daily living. They can then have the entire power and resources of heaven at their disposal to help them live the kind of life Christ wants them to live. That's what Christianity is all about. This is what the gospel message is all about—to become partakers of the divine nature. In this class we will not only learn how to live victorious Christian lives, how to be successful in soul winning and counseling, but how to have peace of mind. In short we will learn how to take God at his word.

Reading now from *The Great Controversy*, pages 621-622, "The season of distress and anguish before us will require a faith that can endure weariness, delay, and hunger—a faith that will not faint though severely tried. The period of probation is granted to all to prepare for that time. Jacob prevailed because he was persevering and determined. His victory is an evidence of the power of importunate prayer. All who will lay hold of God's promises, as he did, and be as earnest and persevering as he was, will succeed as he succeeded. Those who are unwilling to deny self, to agonize before God, to pray long and earnestly for His blessing, will not obtain it. Wrestling with God—how few know what it is! How few have ever had their souls drawn out after God with intensity of desire until every power is on the stretch. When waves of despair which no language can express sweep over the supplicant, how few cling with unyielding faith to the promises of God.

"Those who exercise but little faith now, are in the greatest danger of falling under the power of satanic delusions and the decree to compel the conscience. And even if they endure the test they will be plunged into deeper distress and anguish in the time of trouble, because they have never made it a habit to trust in God. The lessons of faith which they have neglected they will be forced to learn under a terrible pressure of discouragement.

"We should now acquaint ourselves with God by proving His promises. Angels record every prayer that is earnest and sincere. We should rather dispense with selfish gratifications than neglect communion with God. The deepest poverty, the greatest self-denial, with His approval, is better than riches, honors, ease and friendship without it. We must take time to pray. If we allow our minds to be absorbed by worldly interests, the Lord may give us time by removing from us our idols of gold, of houses, or of fertile lands."

It's important to remember that we're in the midst of a great controversy. Satan doesn't like this program. Don't be surprised if things get tough for awhile, but that will only increase dependence upon claiming God's promises and seeing His power made manifest.

Some of the students experience victories of a very personal nature; real battles have been won over self. The love of God, the power of His promises, the growing trust, the changes of character, the complete surrender of self to the will of God, will all be reflected as each student shares their testimony during your sharing time together. As long as we trust the Lord and claim His promises, we will be able to cope with whatever trials we're confronted with. We have found the true spiritual motivation comes only from *living by Christ as He lived by the Father.*—John 6:57. This results in continual victory over sin in our life through His power.

Before you start your actual study you might be encouraged to read God's promises about the promises. Refer to the following texts:

Numbers 11:23; 14:11; 23:19	2 Samuel 7:21
Deuteronomy 4:29, 31	Psalm 50:14, 15
Joshua 21:45	Psalm 56:10, 11

This is what God is helping us to do; to become more acquainted with God by proving his promises. We will get out of this course just exactly what we put into it. Our hope and prayer is that you will learn the need of relying on the promises of God, but more importantly, that you will come to know the Promisor behind the promises. God's peace and blessings.

"Those who accept and obey one of His precepts because it is convenient to do so, while they reject another because its observance would require a sacrifice, lower the standard of right ..."

—*The Sanctified Life,* p. 20

ENDNOTES

Lesson One—The Prayer of Faith

[1] White, Desire of Ages, 622, 2 Peter 1:4

[2] White, Desire of Ages, 200

[3] White, Desire of Ages, 525

[4] White, Education, 257

[5] White, My Life Today, 19

[6] White, Desire of Ages, 348

[7] White, Education, 258

[8] White, Steps to Christ, 51

[9] White, Education, 253

[10] White, Thoughts From the Mount of Blessings, 133

[11] White, Letter, 51

[12] White, Education, 253-261

Lesson Two—Fundamental Principles and Presumption

[13] White, Steps to Christ, 44-45

[14] White, Messages to Young People, 158

[15] White, Christ's Object Lesson, 333

[16] White, Education, 126

[17] White, Thoughts from the Mount of Blessings, 76

[18] White, Christ's Object Lessons, 147-148

[19] White, Ministry of Healing, 159

[20] White, Christ's Object Lessons, 143

[21] White, 1 Selected Messages, 67

[22] White, Christ's Object Lessons, 333

[23] White, Thoughts from the Mount of Blessings, 142

[24] White, My Life Today, 250

[25] White, Messages to Young People, 29

26 White, Education, 257

27 White, Desire of Ages, 429

28 White, Desire of Ages, 126

29 White, My Life Today, 19

30 White, Desire of Ages, 126

31 White, Thoughts from the Mount of Blessings, 146-7

32 White, Thoughts from the Mount of Blessings, 146-7

33 White, Steps to Christ, 96

34 White, Christ Object Lessons, 142

35 White, Steps to Christ, 102

36 White, 2 Testimonies, 157

37 White, Steps to Christ, 93-104

Lesson Three—Conditions to Answered Prayer

38 White, The Faith I live By, 18

39 White, Education, 126

40 White, Education, 258

41 White, Education, 284

42 White, 8 Testimonies, 178

43 White, Desire of Ages, 668

44 White, Christ Object Lessons, 147

45 White, Desire of Ages, 266

46 White, Steps to Christ, 97

47 White, Steps to Christ, 98

48 White, Thoughts from the Mount of Blessings, 20

49 White, Thoughts from the Mount of Blessings, 146

50 White, Christ Object Lessons, 116

51 White, 1 Selected Messages, 375

52 White, Steps to Christ,97

53 White, Our Higher Calling, 151

[54] White, Steps to Christ, 49-55

Lesson Four—Spiritual Living

[55] White, Christ Object Lesson, 147

[56] White, Christ Object Lesson, 147

[57] White, My Life Today, 19

[58] White, Desire of Ages, 259

[59] White, Desire of Ages, 89

[60] White, Christ's Object Lessons, 139-149

Lesson Five—Hindrances To Answered Prayer

[61] White, Message to Young People, 30

[62] White, Christ Object Lessons, 144

[63] White, Christ Object Lessons, 143

[64] White, Christ Object Lessons, 148

[65] White, Christ Object Lessons, 146-7

[66] White, Christ Object Lessons, 143

[67] White, Christ Object Lessons, 145

[68] White, Christ Object Lessons, 142

[69] White, Steps to Christ, 39-45

Lesson Six—Prayer of Commitment

[70] White, Counsels on Health, 375

[71] White, Counsels on Health, 375

[72] White, Counsels on Health, 376-380

[73] White, Education, 108

[74] White, Christ Object Lessons, 84, 85

[75] White, Desire of Ages, 824

[76] White, Counsels on Health, 37

[77] White, Counsels on Health, 324

[78] White, Ministry of Healing, 241

[79] White, Ministry of Healing, 488

[80] White, Ministry of Healing, 249, 251, 253

[81] White, Patriarchs and Prophets, 378

[82] White, Counsels on Health, 37

[83] White, Ministry of Healing, 127

[84] White, Ministry of Healing, 127

[85] White, Ministry of Healing, 128

[86] White, Counsels on Health, 38

[87] White, Ministry of Healing, 227-228

[88] White, Mind, Character, and Personality Vol 2, 264

[89] White, Ministry of Health and Healing, 122-127

Lesson Seven—The Holy Spirit

[90] White, Thoughts from the Mount of Blessings, 27

[91] White, Desire of Ages, 672

[92] White, Help in Daily Living, 7

[93] Life Application Bible, 1503

[94] Life Application Bible, 1387

Lesson Eight—Living For Service

[95] John Ogilvie, God's Best for My Life, July 6

[96] White, 6 Testimonies, 134

[97] White, Education, 53-58

Lesson Nine—How to Have Peace of Mind

[98] White, Letter, 51A 1874

[99] White, Letter, 51A 1874

[100] White, Thought from the Mount of Blessings, 28

[101] White, 2 Selected Messages, 267

[102] White, Thoughts from the Mount of Blessings, 101

[103] White, Ministry of Healing, 471

[104] White, Christ Object Lessons, 146

[105] White, Desire of Ages, 436

[106] White, Christ Object Lessons, 146

[107] White, Patriarchs and Prophets, 596

[108] White, Great Controversy, 555

[109] White, Ministry of Healing, 251

[110] White, Ministry of Healing, 488

[111] White, Ministry of Healing, 249

[112] White, Desire of Ages, 442

[113] White, 2 Testimonies, 506

[114] White, Christ Object Lessons, 172

[115] White, Great Controversy, 622

[116] White, Steps to Christ, 115-128

Lesson Ten—The Relationship of Faith and Prayer

[117] White, Christ Object Lessons, 146

[118] White, In Heavenly Places, 241

[119] White, Christ Object Lessons, 147

[120] White, 1 Testimonies, 699

[121] White, Ministry of Healing, 251

[122] White, Steps to Christ, 80

[123] White, Great Controversy, 622

[124] White, Five Testimonies, 427

[125] White, Ministry of Healing, 122

[126] White, My Life Today, 28

[127] White, Great Controversy, 600

[128] White, Great Controversy, 622

Appendix B

[129] White, Counsels to Parents, Teachers and Students, 31

And we know that all things work together for good to those who love God, to those who are the called according to His purpose. For whom He foreknew, He also predestined to be conformed to the image of His Son, that He might be the firstborn among many brethren.

—Romans 8:28-29

OTHER TITLES BY DR. DERRY JAMES-TANNARIELLO

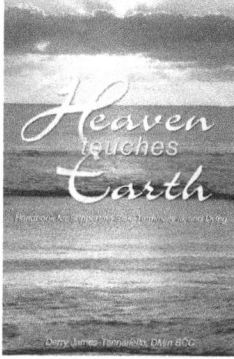

Heaven Touches Earth—Handbook for Supporting Sick, Terminally Il and Dying was written to provide you with the skills and tools necessary to bring solace and comfort to the sick and suffering at home, in the hospital or hospice ministry.

This concise "how-to handbook" is also a succinct resource of clear insight into hospital practices and protocols useful in training volunteers, parish visitors, pastors and chaplains and a helpful refresher guide for those who have studied hospital ministry.

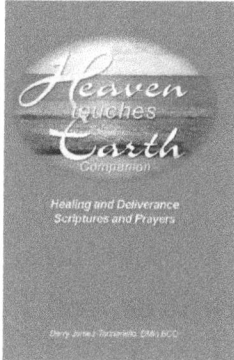

Heaven Touches Earth Companion—Healing and Deliverance Scriptures and Prayers is a take-along resource containing only the Healing and Deliverance Scriptures and Prayers chapter of the **Heaven Touches Earth** book. It is designed for those ministering in a supportive role. (63 pages.)

Both of these books are available in eBook format at Amazon.com or at **FreedomInSurrender.net**.

For gift or bulk orders of these, or any of Derry's books, please visit our website: **FreedomInSurrender.net**

Living Volume One:
Praying in the YES of God

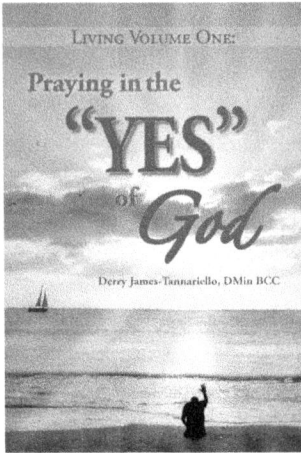

God knows your name! *Do you believe that? Do you believe there even is a God?*

Do you believe that Jesus Christ knows who you are and is interested in your life? Do you believe that He is Who He says He is, and can do what He says He can do?

When you pray, does it sometimes feel like your prayers are hitting the ceiling, or are falling on deaf ears? Are you angry with God because your prayers seem not to be answered? Have you given up asking God for things for yourself because you don't want to be disappointed again; or you're afraid that if God is silent you will begin to question His existence, and then you'll have nothing to put your hope and trust in?

Praying in the YES of God *will help you find those answers and give you the tools to face the unknown with the peace and confidence that God loves you! Learn how to live with triumphant faith, peace of mind, and enthusiastic testimony.*

Available in eBook format at Amazon.com or at **FreedomInSurrender.net**

UPCOMING TITLES

With Gladness Every Day
and
With Kisses from Heaven

A multi-volume compilation of stories from a life lived in service, obedience and total dependence on God and His Mercy—Available 2017.

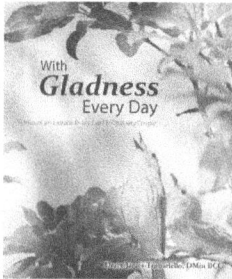

A compilation of stories with Answers to Prayer and Lessons from Scripture and Life Experiences from a life lived in service, obedience and total dependence on God and His Mercy.

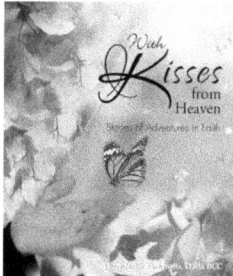

A compilation of stories with Spiritual Application and of God's Intervention from a life lived in surrender, faith, love and total dependence on God and His plans.

DID THIS BOOK BLESS YOU?

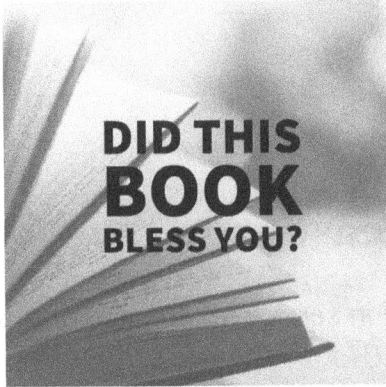

Why Not Bless Others!!!

FreedomInSurrender.net

✓ Mention this book on your social media platforms; use the hashtag: #GrowingInTheYesOfGod

✓ Are you a blogger? Consider writing a book review on your blog. Post it to your blog and other retail book outlets

✓ Know someone else who would be blessed by this book? Pick up a copy for a friend or coworker

✓ Recommend this book to your church library or small group study

✓ Share this message on Facebook. "I was blessed by *Growing in the "YES" of God* by Derry James-Tannariello and Freedom In Surrender Ministries

✓ Follow us on Facebook. Let us know what you like and stay up-to-date on upcoming new releases and pearls of wisdom from Derry!

Facebook.com/FreedomInSurrenderMinistries
@FreedomInSurrender

@PrayWithDerry

/PrayWithDerry

www.ingramcontent.com/pod-product-compliance
Lightning Source LLC
Chambersburg PA
CBHW062039090426

42740CB00016B/2961